Visits to Some

Preston & District Churches & Chapels

c1870

From articles in the *Preston Chronicle*
by Anthony Hewitson ['*Atticus*']

Selected by
Terry Mansfield

Landy Publishing
2010

ISBN: 978 1 872895 81 9
A catalogue record of this book is available from the British Library.

Landy Publishing have also published:--

Northward by Anthony Hewitson
By Rivers, Through Valleys & Dales by Alan Duckworth & Jim Halsall
A History of Pilling by Frank Sobee
Galgate in Focus by Ruth Z Roskell
Glimpses of Glasson Dock by Ruth Z Roskell
Lancashire's Medieval Monasteries by Brian Marshall
Singleton's Story by Singleton Local History Group
Traipsing from a Lancashire Toll Bar by Betty Gilkes & Stan Pickles
Penwortham, Hutton & Longton in Focus by Catherine Rees

A full list may be obtained from
Landy Publishing, 3 Staining Rise, Staining, Blackpool, FY3 0BU
Tel: 01253 895678
Email: landypublishing@yahoo.co.uk

Design by Terry Mansfield

Printed by The Nayler Group, Church. Tel 01254 234247

CONTENTS

**A 19th century engraving of the interior
of St Walburge's Catholic church**

ACKNOWLEDGEMENTS

Thanks are due for the great help we have received in many forms. We are specially grateful to Margaret Dickinson, Andrew Hobbs, David Eaves and The Rev Michael Dolan. The resources of the Talbot Library in Preston were invaluable, as also were the on-line pages of the *Preston Chronicle*, available from the British Library. Martin Duesbury kindly allowed us to use the excellent photograph of his great-grandfather.

INTRODUCTION

Nearly a century after his death in 1912, Anthony Hewitson, author of this book, is getting the attention he deserves. His diaries, held in the Lancashire County Record Office, are being transcribed and his biography is being written. Together, they will reveal that he was a major figure in the story of Preston. A time-served journalist, he became editor and owner of the 'Preston Chronicle', a man of tremendous energy, a *mover and shaker* in pointing out and trying to remedy ills in his adopted home town. He favoured no particular party or religious body, which enabled him to criticise and praise without prejudice.

He was a writer of beautifully descriptive prose and had an unsurpassed command of the English language. Not without cause has he been compared to Charles Dickens, who also observed Preston, which inspired his novel 'Hard Times'. As he walked around Preston, he observed and recorded much that the town could be proud of – and the other side of the coin too.

Travelling by train to such places as Wray Green and Knot End (both now spelled differently), he commented on his fellow passengers, the engines, the porters and on the fact that there were no trains to Pilling on a Sunday, *'not because it was sinful, but because if the trains were run, they would not pay!!'*

This book is made up of pieces which first appeared in the 'Preston Chronicle' in 1869-72, then with little delay in book form:- 'Our Churches & Chapels' (which covered Preston) and 'Our Country Churches & Chapels' (which covered the outlying villages). What these titles don't tell is that they also described the incumbents, priests, ministers, leaders, congregations and organ-blowers. The vicar at St Luke's, who *'smiled but seldom'* had difficulty in giving over preaching when he got to the end. Rev Myres of St Paul's was *'corporeally condensed'* but *'all his sheep have a genial and affectionate bleat for him'* …. *'If cleanliness be next to godliness, a good cleaning would do St Peter's good'* …. *'Few districts are more thoroughly vitiated, more distinctly poverty-struck, more entirely at enmity with soap and water than that in which St Saviour's stands'* …. *'You could not more put a nightcap upon the Catholics of Preston than you could blacken up the eye of the sun.'*

Read on and travel to Preston's past.

PREFACE

In 2005 an announcement appeared on the Internet saying that 'Mystery Worshippers' would visit churches across London, and would report on sermon quality and length, pew comfort, the warmth of the welcome and even the quality of the after-service coffee. All visits would be anonymous, but the assessor would leave a calling card, complete with a picture of the 'Lone Ranger', in the collection plate. This was an extension of a scheme begun in 1998, the brainchild of Steve Goddard, a former marketing executive with Walmart. Goddard was familiar with the use of 'Mystery Shoppers', market research staff posing as customers, to check the quality of service in its stores.

The idea was by no means as original as many of the participants may have believed, for in Preston something very similar began as long ago as the 1860s. At that time most churches enjoyed seemingly impervious positions, and many clergy reigned supreme in society. It must have seemed impudent and thoroughly disrespectful for a provincial journalist to write "parsons must be either sharp or stupid, sensible or foolish; priests must be either learned or illiterate, either good, bad, or indifferent" and "the churches and chapels, with their congregations, must likewise present some points of beauty or ugliness, some traits of grace or godlessness, some features of excellence, dignity, piety, or sham". It was with words like these that Anthony Hewitson, in 1869, using the pseudonym 'Atticus', announced his extraordinary project to inspect and appraise one-by-one all the churches and chapels of Preston, and subsequently to include many of those in the surrounding areas.

This book contains extracts from some of his reports which first appeared in the 'Preston Chronicle', and were soon reprinted in two books in 1869 and 1872. Although readers in Preston and nearby will be particularly interested, and often greatly amused, by comments about their own places of worship and communities, there is much to interest those further afield. He paints a clear picture of the social scene as mirrored in church, for example the delineations arising from pew rents. He was perceptive of divisive forces operating: "A stiff quarrel is about the surest and quickest thing we are acquainted with for multiplying places of worship, for Dissenters, at any rate; and probably it would be found to work with efficacy, if tried, amongst other bodies. Local experience shows that disputes in congregations invariably end in the erection of new chapels. Show us a body of hard, fiercely-quarrelsome religious people, and although neither a prophet nor the son of one, we dare predict that a new place of worship will be the upshot of their contentions." Introducing his authoritative book on Protestantism 'Christianity's Dangerous Idea' [2007] Professor Alister McGrath wrote "The 'dangerous idea' at the heart of Protestantism is that every individual has the right and responsibility to interpret the Bible. With no overarching authority to rein in 'wayward' thought....the spread of this principle has led to five hundred years of remarkable innovation and adaptability — but also to cultural incoherence and instability." Although it was not his principal objective, Hewitson provides a perceptive account of such 'instability', which often began with minor disputes within congregations, swelling into emotional forces masquerading as theological principles sufficient to cause serious rifts.

ANTHONY HEWITSON 1836 - 1912

Anthony Hewitson was born in Blackburn on 13th August 1836. His father was a stonemason who moved to work in Lancaster, and Anthony went to live with his maternal grandparents in Ingleton where he attended school. In 1850 he rejoined his parents in Lancaster and was apprenticed to Mr Clarke, printer and proprietor of the '*Lancaster Gazette*'. In July 1857 he became a reporter and compositor with the '*Kendal Mercury*', then gained wider experience in South Staffordshire with the Brierley Hill Advertiser. After a further move to Wolverhampton, he returned to the north-west in 1858 to a succession of appointments —with the '*Preston Guardian*', the '*Preston Chronicle*' and the '*Preston Herald*' (where he was responsible for the literary and general management). He went back to the *Chronicle* as chief reporter and there, on 28 March 1863, a new weekly column was announced entitled '*Every-Day Gossip About Anything and Anybody Anywhere*'. The author was Hewitson using the pseudonym '*Atticus*', and his opening statement in the first of his columns suggested that he had been given a most extraordinary degree of editorial freedom:

"*…..I shall indulge in gossip; comment upon what takes place at home and abroad; expatiate upon men and manners, politics and ethics, passing events and current topics, sayings and doings, in town and country, in Preston and the neighbourhood, in the United Kingdom alternately, and in all creation periodically. I dislike preliminary soap, but allow me to say that I shall always endeavour to hold the mirror up to nature, and shall submit to no restriction. My platform will be a large one; everything, from patent starch up to the propagation of the Gospel, will, in turn, come under the calligraphy of my grey goose quill. My effusions will assume the shape of a newspaper column of matter; and this I shall keep up every week, except when too ill or too lazy for duty. No editorial responsibility need be incurred on my account….*"

In the Chronicle of July 25th 1863, only four months after the '*Every-Day Gossip*' series had begun, '*Atticus*' felt it necessary to write very provocatively about the activities of some Irishmen who had been appointed as preachers in Preston's churches. This extract provides a distinct foretaste of what was to come when he began his new project in 1869:

"*They are setting the town on fire with their detestable diatribes against the Roman Catholics, and bringing a disgrace upon enlightened Protestantism by their mediaeval attacks upon quiet people, who want to get to heaven according to their own consciences. ……The object of these Irish parsons —indeed the chief aim of all newly extracted Protestants from the other side of the water— seems to be the conversion or rather the denunciation of Roman Catholics. This is the ostensible motive but like many other things they are connected with it is quite possible, that it may only be a 'move.' By creating a hue and cry sensation about the horrors of Popery they expect to get noticed, then praised, then promoted from the poverty-stricken office of curacies into snug incumbencies, where they will soon drop all their incendiarism, and instead of being fire-brands will resolve themselves into the blandest and sleekest of all humdrums —into mere evangelical Falstaffs, with hearts capable of embracing every heretic in the land, and with a cosy hankering after carpet-slippered piety and good dinners. This is the game of the Irish clerical adventurers who are now blacking the eyes of the Pope, and putting thumbscrews on the Roman Catholics of Preston, and trying to revive the days of witch-burning, religious persecution, and bigotry. If the conversion of Papists was their sole—their real object— why didn't they stay in Ireland? There are more Romanists in that country now than they would be able to convert in a cycle of centuries*".

Hewitson was not mounting this attack because of his own allegiancies, for he himself was not a Roman Catholic. It was typical of the desire for justice and fairness which pervaded all his writings.

THE PRESTON  CHRONICLE
AND LANCASHIRE
ADVERTISER.

No. 2959.—PRICE TWOPENCE—[Quarter Due.]   SATURDAY, MARCH 21, 1868.

21 March, 1868 was a pivotal date in Hewitson's life — the Chronicle announced that it would in future be published and edited by him as its new proprietor. In the same issue he made this statement of his intentions:

"With regard to the future, the new proprietor wishes to remark that the Chronicle will be conducted on the same broad and independent principles which have hitherto been recognised by it. Its politics will be eminently Liberal,—eminently on the side of sound and practical progress, with a due regard and respect for all existing institutions which infuse energy and truth into the life of a free people, and give dignity to the constitution of a great nation. The Chronicle will be the organ of no special class in religion. Its motto will be 'FAIR PLAY FOR ALL.' In every matter, whether denominational or political, civil or commercial, the editor will speak right out, freely and fearlessly. His comments will be decisive and clear, on the side of the fullest toleration, the widest improvement, the most unfettered progress. Vigour without violence, manly criticism without scurrility, brisk and cogent argument without bigotry, will be the characteristics of his pen."

Just a year later he launched his most extraordinary project — a new column in the Chronicle was headed:

OUR CHURCHES AND CHAPELS: THEIR PARSONS, PRIESTS AND CONGREGATIONS
BY ATTICUS

He began thus: *"Writing under this nom de plume seems like returning to one's first love —like entering a well-beaten path— like coming home again, and having one's own way for a season."* There was in reality nothing well-beaten about the path he was to take, but he did have much of his own way as he succeeded in visiting services in all the churches and chapels in Preston, and many in the surrounding communities. His comments often breached the embedded dignity of the clergy, and confronted the superficiality of many of the denominational postures which had arisen in the 19th century, some of which persist today.

Anthony Hewitson died on 26th Octber 1912. His obituary in the Preston Guardian made special mention of his book '*Northward*' which is still in print today, of his commentary on the records of the Preston Corporation covering a period of 160 years, and of his '*Illustrative History of Preston*'. Surprisingly, however, there was no mention at all of the two books we intend to cover here—had they been forgotten in the 40 years since their publication? The obituary went on to say *"Mr. Hewitson had travelled much both in America and Europe, and had many interesting reminiscences to tell of Carlyle and other men of genius he had met."* He had *"many personal friends, enjoyed wonderfully robust health up to a comparatively recent date, and his pen was busy almost to the last."* Part of his retirement was spent at his home in Queen's Road, Fulwood, but declining health necessitated his removal to Bare, near Morecambe, where he died. His funeral at Preston Cemetery was conducted by the Rev Benjamin Nightingale of Cannon Street Congregational Church.

From the *Preston Chronicle,* 20th March 1869

It is important that something should be known about our churches and chapels; it is more important that we should be acquainted with their parsons and priests; it is most important that we should have a correct idea of their congregations, for they show the consequences of each, and reflect the character and influence of all. We have a wide field before us. The domain we enter upon is unexplored. Our streets, with their mid-day bustle and midnight sin; our public buildings, with their outside elaboration and inside mysteries; our places of amusement, with their gilded fascinations and shallow delusions; our clubs, bar parlours, prisons, cellars, and workhouses, with their amenities, frivolities, and severities, have all been commented upon; but the most important of our institutions, the best, the queerest, the solemnest, the oddest—the churches and chapels of the town—have been left out in the cold entirely.

There are about 45 churches and chapels and probably 60 parsons and priests in Preston; but unto this hour they have been treated, so far as they are individually concerned, with complete silence. We propose remedying the defect, supplying the necessary criticism, and filling up the hiatus. The whole lot must have either something or nothing in them, must be either useful or useless; parsons must be either sharp or stupid, sensible or foolish; priests must be either learned or illiterate, either good, bad, or indifferent; in all, from the rector in his silken gown to the back street psalm-singer in his fustian, there must be something worth praising or condemning. And the churches and chapels, with their congregations, must likewise present some points of beauty or ugliness, some traits of grace or godlessness, some features of excellence, dignity, piety, or sham. There must be either a good deal of gilded gingerbread or a great lot of the genuine article, at our places of worship. But whether there is or there is not, we have decided to say something about the church and the chapel, the parson and the priest, of each district in the town.

All the churches and chapels of the land may profess Christianity; but the game of the bulk has a powerful reference to money. Those who have got the most of the current coin of the realm receive the blandest smile from the parson........ those who have not got it must take what they can get, and accept it with Christian resignation, as St. Paul tells them. This may be all right; we have not said yet that it is wrong; but it looks suspicious, doesn't it?—shows that in the arena of conventional Christianity, as in the seething maelstrom of ordinary life, money is the winner.

Priests are not as jolly as they once were.....the parsons of the past were also a blithesome set of individuals. They were perhaps rougher than those mild and refined gentlemen who preach now-a-days; but they were straightforward, thorough, absolutely English, well educated, and stronger in the brain than many of them. In each Episcopalian, Catholic, and Dissenting community there are now some most erudite, most useful men; but if we take the great multitude of them, and compare their circumstances—their facilities for education, the varied channels of usefulness they have—with those of their predecessors, it will be found that the latter were the cleverer, often the wiser, and always the merrier men.

Plainness, erudition, blithesomeness, were their characteristics. Aye, look at our modern men given up largely to threnody-chiming and to polishing off tea and muffin with elderly females, and compare them, say, for instance, with—

> The poet Praed's immortal Vicar,
> Who wisely wore the cleric gown,
> Sound in theology and liquor;
> Quite human, though a true divine,
> His fellow-men he would not libel;
> He gave his friends good honest wine,
> And drew his doctrine from the Bible.

Institute a comparison, and then you will say that whilst modern men may be very aesthetic and neatly dressed, the ancient apostolic successors, though less refined, had much more metal in them, were more kindly, genial; and told their followers to live well, to eat well, and to mind none of the hair-splitting neological folly which is now cracking up Christendom.

In old times the Lord did not 'call' so many parsons from one church to another as it is said He does now; in the days which have passed the bulk of subordinate parsons did not feel a sort of conscientious hankering every three years for an 'enlarged sphere of usefulness,' where the salary was proportionately increased. We have known multitudes of parsons, in our time, who have been 'called' to places where their salaries were increased; we know of but few who have gravitated to a church where the salary was less than the one left. 'Business' enters largely into the conceptions of clergymen. As a rule, no teachers of religion, except Catholic priests and Methodist ministers, leave one place for another where less of this world's goods and chattels predominate; and *they* are *compelled* to do so, else the result might be different. When a priest gets his mittimus he has to budge; it is not a question of '*he said or she said,*' but of—go; and when a Wesleyan is triennially told to either look after the interests of a fresh circuit or retire into space, he has to do so. It would be wrong to say that lucre is at the bottom of every parsonic change; but it is at the foundation of the great majority—eh? If it isn't, just make an inquiry, as we have done.

We should have scarcely been doing justice to the matter if we had not had a quiet '*fling*' at the money part of it. In the letters which will follow this, we shall deal disinterestedly with all. Our object will be to present a picture of things as they are, and to avoid all meddling with creeds. People may believe what they like, so far as we are concerned, if they behave themselves, and pay their debts. It is utterly impossible to get all to be of the same opinion; creeds, like faces, must differ, have differed, always will differ; and the best plan is to let people have their own way so long as it is consistent with the general welfare of social and civil life.

The first contribution, about Preston Parish Church, appeared on 27th March 1869, and thirty-seven more appeared weekly until that on St Mary's (beginning 'And now, finally, brethren') on 11th December 1869. The total content amounted to over 100,000 words. In the *Chronicle* of 11th December there was an advertisement:

The Parish Church of St John the Divine
(now called 'Preston Minster')

Taking the congregation of our Parish Church in the aggregate, it is a fair sample of every class of human life. You have the old maid carrying a Prayer Book belonging to a past generation; you have the ancient bachelor with plenty of money and possessing a thorough knowledge as to the safest way of keeping it, his great idea being that the best way of getting to heaven is to stick to his coins, attend church every Sunday, and take the sacrament regularly; you have the magistrate, whose manner, if not his beard, is of formal cut; the retired tradesman, with his domestic-looking wife, and smartly-dressed daughters, ten times finer than ever their mother was; the manufacturer absorbed in cotton; the lawyer, who has carried on a decent business amongst fees during the week, and has perhaps turned up to join in the general confession; the pushing tradesman, who has to live by going to church, as well as by counter work; the speculating shopkeeper, who has a connection to make; the young finely-feathered lady, got up in silk and velvet; the dandy buttoned up to show his figure, and heavily dosed with scent; the less developed young swell, who is always *'talking about his pa and his ma,'* and has only just begun to have his hair parted down the middle; the broken down middle-aged man who was once in a good position, but who years since went all in a piece to pot; the snuff-loving old woman who curtsies before fine folk, who has always a long tale to tell about her sorrows, and who is periodically consoled by a *'trifle;'* the working man who is rather a scarce article, except upon special occasions; and the representative of the poorest class, living somewhere in that venal slum of slime and misery behind the church.

A considerable number of those floating beings called *'strags'* attend the Parish Church. They go to no place regularly; they gravitate at intervals to the church, mainly on the ground that their fathers and mothers used to go there, and because they were christened there; but they belong to a cunning race; they can scent the battle from afar, and they generally keep about three-quarters of a mile from the Parish Church when a collection has to be made. ..... *"What's the reason there are so few people here?"* ..... *"There's a collection and the 'strags' won't take the bait."* It is the same more or less at every place of worship; and to tell the truth, there's a sort of instinctive dislike of collections in everybody's composition.

Canon Parr, the 17th Vicar of St John's

Canon Parr is an easy-going, genial, educated man kindly disposed towards good living, not blessed with over much money, fond of wearing a billycock, and strongly in love with a cloak. He has seen much of the world, is shrewd, has a long head, has both studied and travelled for his learning, and is the smartest man Preston Protestants could have to defend their cause. But he has a certain amount of narrowness in his mental vision, and, like the bulk of parsons, can see his own way best. He has a strong temper within him, and he can redden up beautifully all over when his equanimity is disturbed. If you tread upon his ecclesiastical bunions he will give you either a dark mooner or an eye opener—we use these classical terms in a figurative sense. He will keep quiet so long as you do; but if you make an antagonistic move he will punish you if possible. He can wield a clever pen; his style is cogent, scholarly, and, unless overburdened with temper, dignified. He can fling the shafts of satire or distil the balm of pathos; can be bitter, saucy, and aggravating; can say a hard thing in a cutting style; and if he does not go to the bone it's no fault of his. He can also tone down his language to a point of elegance and tenderness; can express a good thing excellently, and utter a fine sentiment well. His speaking is modelled after a good style; but it is inferior to his writing. In the pulpit he expresses himself easily, often fervently, never rantingly. The pulpit of the Parish Church will stand for ever before he upsets it, and he will never approach that altitude of polemical phrenitis which will induce him to smash any part of it. His pulpit language is invariably well chosen; some of his subjects may be rather commonplace or inappropriate, but the words thrown into their exposition are up to the mark.

He seldom falters; he has never above one, "*and now, finally, brethren,*" in his concluding remarks; he invariably gives over when he has done—a plan which John Wesley once said many parsons neglected to observe; and his congregation, whether they have been awake or fast asleep, generally go away satisfied.

The Rev. J. T. Brown of Holy Trinity Church

About two years ago, when he came to the church the congregation was wretchedly thin—awfully scarce, and just on the borders of invisibility. It has since improved a little; but working up a forsaken place into real activity is a difficult task, which at times staggers the ablest of men. Mr. Brown is a scholar, and a thoroughly upright man. He believes not in fighting down other people's creeds; never rails against religious antagonists; has a natural dislike to platform bigotry and pulpit wrathfulness; is generously inclined; will give but not lend; objects to everything in the shape of loud clerical display; is strongly evangelical in his tastes; is exact, and calm, and orderly, even to the cut of his whiskers; won't be brought out and exhibited; doesn't care about seeing other people make exhibitions. But he is far too good for a parson. He always preaches sincerely; a quiet spirit of simple unadorned, piety pervades his remarks—but he depresses you too much; and is rather predisposed to a calm mournful consideration of the great sulphur question. He never gets into a lurid passion, never horrifies, but calmly saddens you, in his discourses.

Christ Church

Nobody has yet said that Christ Church, architecturally, is a very nice place; and we are not going to say so. It is a piece of calm sanctity in buckram, is a stout mass of undiluted limestone, has been made ornate with pepper castors, looks sweetly-clean after a summer shower, is devoid of a steeple, will never be blown over, couldn't be lifted in one piece, and will nearly stand forever.

The first incumbent of Christ Church was the Rev. T. Clark—a kindly-exact, sincere, quiet-moving gentleman, who did much good in his district, visited poor people regularly, wasn't afraid of going down on his knees in their houses, gave away much of that which parsons and other sinners generally like to keep—money, and was greatly respected. We shall always remember him—remember him for his quaint, virtuous preciseness, his humble, kindly plodding ways,..... his dislike of having '*e*' put after his name, and his courteous, accomplished, affable manners. He was succeeded by his son-in-law, the Rev. Raywood Firth. A few years ago Mr. Firth visited Preston as secretary of a society in connection with the Church of England; then got married to the daughter of the Rev. T. Clark; subsequently became curate of that gentleman's church; and in 1864 was made its incumbent. Well done! The ascent is good. We like the transition. Mr. Firth likes visiting folk who are well off; wouldn't object to tea, crumpet, and conversation with the better end of his flock any day; visits fairly in his district, and says many

a good word to folk in poverty, but would look at a floor before going down upon it like his predecessor; thinks that flags and boards should be either very clean or carpeted before good trousers touch them; might advantageously mix up with the poor of his district a little more. His salary is about £400 a year, and that is a sum which the generality of people would not object to. In the pulpit he never gets either fast asleep or hysterical. He can preach good original sermons—carefully worked out, well-balanced, neatly arranged; and he can give birth to some which are rather dull and mediocre. ...... He is not a, '*gatherer and disposer of other men's stuff,*' like some clerical greengrocers: what he says is his own, and he sticks to it.

> The 'latest thing' may be seen in hair, and bonnets, and dresses

The superior members of the congregation, as a rule, gravitate downwards, have seats on the ground floor,—it is vulgar to sit in the galleries. They are all excellently attired; the '*latest thing*' may be seen in hair, and bonnets, and dresses; the best of coats and the cleanest of waistcoats are also observable. The congregation is substantial in look, and possesses many excellent qualities; but there is a great amount of what Dr. Johnson would call '*immiscibility*' in it. Nearly every part of it has a very strong notion that it is better than any other part. The congregation at Christ Church won't mix itself up; is fond of '*distance*'; says, in a genteely pious tone, '*keep off*'; can't be approached beyond a certain point; isn't sociable; won't stand any hand-shaking except in its own peculiar circles.

St. George's Church

St. George's was erected in 1723. Up to that time the Parish Church was the only place of worship we had in connection with what is termed '*the Establishment;*' St. George's was brought into existence as a '*chapel of ease*' for it; and it is still one of the easiest, quietest, best behaved places in the town. It was a plain brick edifice at the beginning, but in 1843-4 the face of the church was hardened—it was turned into stone, and it continues to have a substantial petrified appearance.

No place of worship can in its internal arrangements be much plainer than St. George's. If it were not for three stained windows in the chancel, which you can but faintly make out at a distance, nothing which could by any possibility be termed ornamental would at first sight strike you. You see a magnificent organ which compensates for multitudes of defects, and below it—in front of the orchestra—a rather powerful representation of the royal arms, a massive lion and unicorn, '*fighting for the crown*' as usual, and got up in polished wood work. We see no reason why there should not be something put up contiguously, emblematic of St. George and the dragon. It is very unfair to the saint and unjust to the dragon to ignore them altogether. There is a quiet, secluded coziness about the pews; the sides are high; the fronts come up well; nobody can see much of you if care is taken; and a position favourable to either recumbent ease or horizontal sleep may be assumed in several of them with safety.

There is no Sunday school in connection with St. George's. In some respects this may be a disadvantage to the neighbourhood; but it is a source of comfort to the congregation, for all the noise which irrepressible children create during service hours at every place where they are penned up, is obviated. Neither children nor babes are seen at St. George's. It is considered they are best at home, and that they ought to stay there until the second teeth have been fairly cut. The congregation of St. George's is specifically fashionable. A few poor people may be seen on low seats in the centre aisle; but the great majority of worshippers either represent, or are connected with, what are termed '*good families.*' Young ladies wearing on just one hair the latest of bonnets, and elaborated with costly silks and ribbons; tender gentlemen of the silver-headed cane school and the '*my deah fellah*' region; quiet substantial looking men of advanced years, who believe in good breeding and properly brushed clothes; elderly matrons, '*awfully spiff;*' and a few well-disposed tradespeople who judiciously mingle piety with business, and never make startling noises during their devotional moments—these make up the congregational elements of St. George's. They may be described in three words—few, serene, select. The worshippers move in high spheres; the bulk of them toil not, neither do they spin; and if they can afford it they are quite justified in making life genteel and easy, and giving instructions for other people to wait upon them.

13

St. Luke's Church

It is in a queer, far-off unshaven region. Aged sparrows and men who like ale better than their mothers, dwell in its surroundings; phalanxes of young Britons, born without head coverings, and determined to keep them off; columns of wives, beautiful for ever in their unwashedness, and better interpreters of the 28th verse of the 1st chapter of Genesis then all the Biblical commentators put together, occupy its district.

The church will accommodate 800 persons. Three-fourths of the sittings are free. The average attendance on Sundays, including school children, is 250. Considering that there are about 5,500 persons in the district, this number is only trifling. When we visited the church there were 280 present, and out of this number 160 were children. We fancied that the weather, for it was rather unfavourable, might have kept many away, but when we recollected that we had passed groups of men standing idly at contiguous street corners, discussing the merits of dogs and ale, as we walked to the church; and saw at least 40 young fellows within a good stone's throw of it as we left, hanging about drinking-house sides, in the drizzling rain, waiting for '*opening time*,' and talking coolly about '*half gallons*,' we grew doubtful as to the correctness of our supposition. If men could bear a quiet drenching in the streets, could leave their homes for the purpose of congregating on the sides of parapets, in order to make a descent upon places essentially '*wet*,' we fancied that moderately inclement weather could not, after all, be set down as the real reason for a thin congregation at St. Luke's.

The congregation worshipping at St. Luke's is formed chiefly of working people. The scholars seem to be of a rather active turn of mind, for in their management they keep two or three men and a female hard at work, and continue after all to have a fair amount of their own way—not, perhaps, quite so much of it as three youths who sat before us, who appeared to extract more pleasure out of some verses on a tobacco paper than out of either the hymns or the sermon.

The incumbent of St. Luke's, the Rev. W. Winlaw, has strong convictions; couldn't be easily persuaded off a notion after once seeing it in his own light; seems to have smiled but seldom; is vigorous when roused, maidenly when cool, cutting when vexed, meek when in smooth water; is generally exact in composition, and clear in style; but preaches rather long sermons, and has a difficulty in giving over when he has got to the end. In one of his sermons we heard him say, after a five-and-twenty minutes run, '*In conclusion*,' '*Lastly*,' and '*Finally*;' and we had almost made up our mind for another sermon after he had '*finished*' but he decided to give over without preaching it.

This engraving appeared in the Preston Chronicle when St Luke's Church was consecrated in 1859

St James' Church

There is a touch of smooth piety and elegance in the name of St. James. It sounds refined, serious, precise. Two of the quietest and most devoted pioneers of Christianity were christened James; the most fashionable quarters in London are St. James'; the Spaniards have for ages recognised St. James as their patron saint; and on the whole whether referring to the '*elder*' or the '*less*' James, the name has a very good and Jamesly bearing. An old English poet says that '*Saint James gives oysters*' just as St. Swithin attends to the rain; but we are afraid that in these days he doesn't look very minutely after the bivalve part of creation: if he does he is determined to charge us enough for ingurgitation, and that isn't a very saintly thing. He may be an ichthyofagic benefactor only—we don't see the oysters as often as we could like. Not many churches are called after St. James, and very few people swear by him. We have a church in Preston dedicated to the saint; but it got the name whilst it was a kind of chapel.

"*Who erected the building?*" said we one day to a churchman, and the curt reply, with a neatly curled lip, was, "*A parcel of Dissenters.*" St. James's was erected by the Rev. James Fielding and his friends. The first stone was laid by Mr. Fielding, May 24th, 1837, and the place was opened for divine worship in January, 1838, under the denomination of '*The Primitive Episcopal Church*'. Not long afterwards Mr. Fielding had a severe attack of illness, and was laid aside from his work. From this, together with the urgency of the contractors for the payment of their bills, it was thought advisable to sell the premises. The Vicar of Preston, in conjunction with his friends, offered £1,000 for the building. This was believed to be considerably under its real value, being £500 below the cost amount. However, under the circumstances it was decided to accept the offer.

The internal architecture of the building is dull and modest. The seats are stiff, between 30 and 40 inches high, and homely. They have a scraped care-worn look, as if they had been getting parish relief. A considerable sum of money was once spent upon the cleaning and renovation of the church; but the paint which was put on during the work never suited; it was either brushed on too thickly or varnished too coarsely; it persisted in sticking to people rather too keenly at times; would hardly give way if struggled with; and taking into account its tenacity and ill-looks —it was finally decided to rub it off, make things easy with pumice stone, and agitate for fresh paint and varnish when the opportunity presented itself.

On the side we noticed seventeen free pews. How many people do you think there were in them? Just one delicious old woman, who wore a brightly-coloured old shawl, and a finely-spreading old bonnet, which in its weight and amplitude of trimmings seemed to frown into evanescence the sprightly half-ounce head gearing of today. Paying for what they get and giving a good price for it when they have a chance is evidently an axiom with the believers in St. James's. There is at present a demand for seats worth from 7s. to 10s. each; but those which can be obtained for 1s. are not much thought of, and nobody will look on one side at the pews which are offered for nothing. That which is not charged for is never cared for; and further, in respect to free pews, patronage of them is an indication of poverty, and people, as a rule, don't like to show the white feather in that department.

nobody will look .... at the pews which are offered for nothing

15

St Mary's Church

St. Mary's is one of those churches which can be felt rather than seen. Until you get quite to it you hardly know you are at it. Approaching it from the west the first glimmering of it you have is over one end of the House of Correction. At this point you catch what seems to be a cluster of crosses —the surmountings of the tower; visions of a ponderous cruet-stand, of five nine pins, and other cognate articles, then strike you; afterwards the body of the church broadens slowly into view, and having described three-fourths of a wide circle with your feet, and passed through a strong gateway, it is found you are at the building.

At the southern end there is a large gallery, overshadowing the noisiest galaxy of Sunday infants we ever encountered. There are more infants at St. Mary's schools than at any other place in Preston, and trouble, combined with vexation of spirit, must consequently exist there in the same ratio. The bulk are kept from the church; but a few manage to creep in, and when we saw them they were having a very happy time of it. Some whistled a little —but they seemed to be only learners and couldn't get on very well with tunes; others tossed halfpennies about, a few operated upon the floor with marbles, and all of them were exceedingly lively.

The members of the choir, to whom several people in the bottom of the church look up periodically, as if trying to find out either what they were doing or how they were dressed, are only in embryo. They are new singers; but some of them have fair voices, and in spite of occasional irregularity in tune and time, they get along agreeably. The elements of a good choir are within them, and they have only to persevere, in order to secure excellence, saying nothing of medals, and other tokens of appreciation.

The Rev. George Alker, who came to St. Mary's in December, 1857, is an Irishman, about 42 years of age. After leaving Ireland, he took a curacy in Liverpool, then he accepted a similar post at St. Peter's, Preston. Here he organised a class of young men, 800 strong, and whilst here he set the town on fire with anti-Popery denunciation. Yes, he was a regular Mr. Blazeaway, and what he said was equal to the strongest of the theatre thunder and the most dazzling of forked lightning. After piling up the agony for a few months at St. Peter's, Mr. Alker left for Dublin, stayed there a short time, then retraced his steps to Preston, and in due time got the incumbency of St. Mary's —an event which seems to have toned down all his fury about the *'abomination of Rome,'* and made him nearly quite forget the existence of Pope Pius. Still he has occasional spells of anti-Popery hysteria; he can't altogether get the old complaint out of his bones; Rome is yet his red rag when in a rage; and he has latterly shown an inclination to wind up the clocks of the Jews and the Mahommedans. He may have a fling at the Calmuck Tartars and a quiet pitch into the Sioux Indians after a bit.

When Mr. Alker first went to St. Mary's his salary was small; but it has now reached the general panacea of incumbents, £300 a year. He has been an energetic worker, and in connection with the schools particularly he has been most useful. For his services in this respect he deserves much praise, and we tender him our share. His influence is hardly so great as it used to be, still he is the great Brahmin and the grand Lama of the locality.

16

St. Paul's Church

The first stone of St. Paul's Church was laid on Tuesday, 21st October, 1823. Out of the million pounds granted by Parliament for the erection of churches, some time prior to the date given, Preston, through Dr. Lawe, who was then Bishop of Chester, got £12,500. It was originally intended to expend this sum in the erection of one church—St. Peter's; but at the request of the Rev. R. Carus Wilson, vicar of Preston, the money was divided, one half going to St. Peter's, and the other to St. Paul's. Some people might consider this like '*robbing Peter to pay Paul*,' but it was better to halve the money for the benefit of two districts, than give all of it for the spiritual edification of one, and leave the other destitute.

The Rev. W. M. Myres came to St.Paul's at the beginning of 1867, and when he made his appearance fidgetty and orthodox souls were in a state of mingled dudgeon and trepidation as to what be would do. It was fancied that he was a Ritualist—fond of floral devices and huge candles, with an incipient itching for variegated millinery, beads, and crosses. But his opponents, who numbered nearly two-thirds of the congregation,

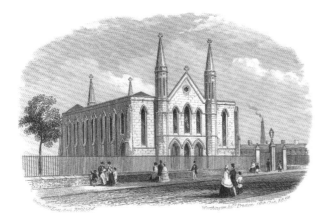

screamed before they were bitten, and went into solemn paroxysms of pious frothiness for nothing. Subsequent events have proved how highly imaginative their views were. No church in the country has less of Ritualism in it than St. Paul's. Its services are pre-eminently plain; all those parts whereon the spirit of innovation has settled so strongly in several churches during the past few years are kept in their original simplicity; and in the general proceedings nothing can be observed calculated to disturb the peace of the most fastidious of show-disliking Churchmen.

Mr. Myres is about 30 years of age, is corporeally condensed, walks as if he were in earnest and wanted to catch the train; has keen powers of observation, has a better descriptive than logical faculty, is not very imaginative, cares more for prose than poetry, more for facts than sallies of the fancy, more for gentle devotion, and quiet persevering labour in his own locality than for virtuous welterings and sacred acrobatism in other districts. He has endeavoured, since coming to Preston, to mind his own business, and parsons often find that a hard thing to accomplish. Polished in education, he is humble and social in manner. If he ever gets into a sacred disturbance the fault will be through somebody else dragging him into it, and not because he has courted it by natural choice. His brain may lack high range and large creativeness; but he possesses qualities of heart and spirit which mere brilliance cannot secure, and which simple cerebral strength can never impart. We admire him for his courteousness, his artless simplicity of nature, his earnest, kindly-devotedness to duty, and his continual attention to everything affecting the welfare of those he has to look after. Mr. Myres is greatly respected by all in his district; and all his sheep have a genial and affectionate bleat for him.

St Peter's Church

St. Peter's Church, internally, looks dirty. If cleanliness be next to godliness, a good cleaning would do it good and improve its affinities. Whitewash, paint, floorcloths, dusters, wash leathers, and sundry other articles in the curriculum of scrubbers, renovators, and purifiers are needed. The walls want mundifying, so does the ceiling, so do the floors; the Ten Commandments need improving; the Apostles' Creed isn't plain enough; the spirit of a time-worn grimness requires ostracising from the place. All is substantial; but there is an ancient unwashed dullness about the general establishment, which needs transforming into cleanness and brightness.

The price of a single sitting in the middle aisle is 10s. per annum; the cost of a side seat is equal to three civil half-crowns. The long side seats are free; so are the galleries, excepting that portion of them in front of the organ. Often the church is not much more than half filled on a Sunday; but it is said that many sittings, calculated to accommodate nearly a full congregation, are let. Viewed from the copperhead standpoint this is right; but taking a higher ground it would be more satisfactory if even fewer pews were let and more folk attended.

The incumbent is the Rev. D. F. Chapman. He has been at the place a few years, and receives about £400-a-year for his trouble. Mr. Chapman is a powerfully-constructed gentleman; is somewhat inclined to oleaginousness; has contracted a marine swing in his walk; is heavily clerical in countenance and cloth; believes in keeping his hair broad at the sides; has a strong will and an enormous opinion of the incumbent of St. Peter's; will fume if crossed; will crush if touched; can't be convinced; has his mind made up and rivetted down on everything; must have his way; thinks every antagonist mistaken; is washy, windy, ponderous; has a clear notion that each of his postulates is worth a couple of demonstrations, that all his theories are tantamount to axioms; and, finally, has quarrelled more with his churchwardens than any other live parson in Preston. He once fought for weeks, day and night, with a warden as to the position of a small gas-pipe, because he couldn't get his way about it. He is well educated, but his erudition is not fairly utilised; he can read with moderate precision; but there is a lack of elocutionary finish in his tone; he can talk a long while, and now and then can say a good thing; he preaches with considerable force, makes good use of his arms, sometimes rants a little, at intervals has to pull back his sentences half an inch to get hold of the right word, talks straight out occasionally, telling the congregation what they are doing and what they ought to do; but there is much in his sermons which neither gods nor men will care about digesting, and there is a theological dogmatism in them which ordinary sinners like ourselves will never swallow.

> The Rev. D. F. Chapman quarrelled more with his churchwardens than any other live parson in Preston

St Saviour's Church

Few districts are more thoroughly vitiated, more distinctly poverty-struck, more entirely at enmity with soap and water than that in which this church stands. Physically, mentally, and spiritually, it is in a state of squash and mildew. Heathenism seethes in it, and something even more potent than a forty-parson power of virtue will be required to bring it to healthy consciousness and legitimate action. You needn't go to the low slums of London, needn't smuggle yourself round with detectives into the back dens of big cities if you want to see '*sights*' of poverty and depravity; you can have them nearer home—at home—in the murky streets, sinister courts, crowded houses, dim cellars, and noisy drinking dens of St. Saviour's district. Pass through it, move quietly along its parapets, and you will see enough to convince you that many missionaries, with numerous Bibles and piles of blankets, are yet wanted at home before being despatched to either farthest Ind or the plains of Timbuctoo.

> Myriads of children, ragged, sore-headed, bare-legged, dirty, and amazingly alive

The general scene may be thus condensed and described: Myriads of children, ragged, sore-headed, bare-legged, dirty, and amazingly alive amid all of it; wretched-looking matrons, hugging saucy, screaming infants to their breasts, and sending senior youngsters for either herring, or beer, or very small loaves; strong, idle young men hanging about street corners with either dogs at their feet, or pigeon-baskets in their hands; little shops driving a brisk '*booking*' business with either females wearing shawls over their heads or children wearing nothing at all on their feet; bevvies of brazen-faced hussies looking out of grim doorways for more victims and more drink; stray soldiers struggling about beer or dram shops entrances, with dissolute, brawny-armed females; and wandering old hags with black eyes and dishevelled hair, closing up the career of shame and ruin they have so long and so wretchedly run.

No locality we know of stands more in need of general redemption than this, and any Christian church, no matter whatever may be its denominational peculiarities, which may exist in it, deserves encouragement and support. The district is so supremely poor, and so absolutely bad, that anything calculated to improve or enlighten it in any way is worthy of assistance.

The congregation, considering the capacity of the church, is large, and consists almost absolutely of working people. We noticed what we have seen at no other church or chapel in the town, namely, that many of the worshippers put in an early appearance —several were in their seats at least a quarter of an hour before the service commenced. We further noticed that the congregation is a pre-eminently quiet and orderly one. At some places you are tormented to death with stirring feet, shuffling, rustling clothes, coughing, sneezing, &c.; here, however, you have little of these things, and at times, a positive dead calm prevails. It may also be worthy of mention that we saw fewer sleepers at St. Saviour's than in any other place of worship yet visited by us. Only one gentleman got fairly into a state of slumber during the whole service; a stout girl tried to '*drop over*' several times, and an old man made two or three quiet efforts to get his eyes properly closed, but both failed. All the other members of the congregation appeared to be wide awake and amazingly attentive. The free seats are well patronised by poor people, and it is to such a class as this that the place seems really advantageous.

Preston's Catholics

It was at one time of the day a rather dangerous sort of thing for a man, or a woman, or a medium-sized infant, living in this highly-favoured land of ours, to show any special liking for Roman Catholicism. But the days of religious bruising have perished; and Catholics are now, in the main, considered to be human as well as other people, and to have a right to live, and put their Sunday clothes on, and go to their own places of worship like the rest of mortals. No doubt there are a few distempered adherents of the *'immortal William'* school who would like to see Catholics driven into a corner, banished, or squeezed into nothing; probably there are some of the highly sublimated *'no surrender'* gentlemen who would be considerably pleased if they could galvanise the old penal code and put a barrel able to play the air of *'Boyne Water'* into every street organ; but the great mass of men have learned to be tolerant, and have come to the conclusion that Catholics, civilly and religiously, are entitled to all the liberty which a free and enlightened constitution can confer —to all the privileges which fair-play and even-handed justice can give; and if these are not fully granted now, the day is coming when they will be possessed. Lancashire seems to be the great centre of Catholicism in England, and Preston appears to be its centre in Lancashire. This benign town of Preston, with its fervent galaxy of lecturing curates, and its noble army of high falutin' incumbents, is the very fulcrum and lever of northern Romanism. If Catholics are wrong and on the way to perdition and blisters there are 33,000 of them here moving in that very awkward direction at the present. A number so large, whether right or wrong cannot be despised; a body so great, whether good or evil, will, by its sheer inherent force, persist in living, moving, and having, a fair share of being. You can't evaporate 33,000 of anything in a hurry; and you could no more put a nightcap upon the Catholics of Preston than you could blacken up the eye of the sun.

St. Wilfrid's Catholic Church is situated in a somewhat sanctified place — Chapel Street; but as about half of that locality is taken up with lawyers' offices, and the centre of it by a police station, we fancy that this world, rather than the next, will occupy the bulk of its attention. It is to be hoped that St. Wilfrid's, which stands on the opposite side, will act as a healthy counterpoise —will, at any rate, maintain its own against such formidable odds. The building in Chapel Street, dedicated to the old Anglo-Saxon bishop —St. Wilfrid— who was a combative sort of soul, fond of argumentatively knocking down obstreperous kings and ecclesiastics and breaking up the strongholds of paganism, was opened seventy-six years ago. There is nothing worth either laughing or crying about so far as its exterior goes. It doesn't look like a church; it resembles not a chapel; and it seems too big for a house. No place of worship in Preston is so finely decorated, so skilfully painted, so artistically got up. Those who have had the management and support of St. Wilfrid's in their hands, have studied the theory of colour to perfection, and whilst we may not theologically agree with some of its uses, one cannot but admire its general effect. Saints, angels, rings, squares, floriations, spiralizations, and everything which the brain or the brush of the most devoted painter could fairly devise are depicted in this church, and there is such an array of them that one wonders how anybody could ever have had the time or patience to finish the work.

the great mass of men have learned to be tolerant

St. Ignatius' Catholic Church

Catholicism owes much to the Jesuits; and, casuistically speaking, the Jesuits owe their existence to a broken leg. Ignatius of Loyola was their founder. He was at first a page, then a soldier, then got one of his legs broken in battle, was captured and confined as an invalid, had his immortal leg set and re-set, whiled away his time whilst it was mending in reading romances, got through all within his reach, could at last find nothing but the '*Lives of the Saints*', had his latent religious feelings stirred during their perusal, travelled to different places afterwards, and at last established the order of Jesuits —an order which has more learning within its circle than perhaps any other section of men, which has sent out its missionaries to every clime, has been subjected to every kind of vicissitude, has been suppressed by kings and emperors, ostracised by at least one Pope, and shouted down often by excited peoples in the heated moments of revolution; but which has somehow managed to live through it all and progress.

In Preston we have three churches, besides an auxiliary chapel, wherein priests of the Jesuit order labour. By far the largest number of Preston Catholics are in charge of those priests, and the generality of them don't seem to suffer anything from the '*tyranny*'—that is the phrase some of us Protestants delight to honour—of their supervision. They can breathe, and walk about, laugh, and grow fat without any difficulty, and they are sanguine of being landed in ultimate ecstasy if they conduct themselves fairly.

The Catholics in the district of this church are very strong; they number about 6,000; are mainly of a working-class complexion; and are conveniently and compactly located for educational and religious purposes. Catholics are so numerous in the neighbourhood—are so woven and interwoven amongst the denizens of it—that it is a good and a safe plan never to begin running down the Pope in any part of it. Murphyites and patent Christians fond of immolating Rome, &c., would have a very poor chance of success in this district.

Human nature, as a rule, can't stand a very long fire of anything, doesn't like to have even too much goodness pushed upon it for too long a time, believes in a very short and very sweet thing. It may have to pay more for it, as it has at the ten o'clock mass on a Sunday, at St. Ignatius'—for the price of seats at that time is just double what it is at any other; only the work is got through sharply, and that is something to be thankful for.

Father Walker is a locomotive, wiry, fibrous man—full of energy, wide awake,—tenacious, keenly perceptive; could pass his sharp eye round you in a second and tell your age, weight, and habits. He has been at St. Ignatius's for two-and-a-half years; the decorations in the church are mainly due to him; and he has earned the respect and affection of the people. His style of preaching is clear, sonorously-sounding, and vigorous—is not rhetorically flashy, but strong, impetuous, and full of energy. He is a clear-headed, determined, sagacious man, and would be formidable, if put to it, with either his logic or fists.

Father Walker

St Mary's Catholic Chapel — Origins

Unless it be our Parish Church, which was originally a Catholic place of worship, no religious building in Preston possesses historic associations so far-reaching as St. Mary's. It is the oldest Catholic chapel in Preston. Directly, it is associated with a period of fierce persecution. After the dissolution, caused by Henry VIII, it was a dangerous thing to profess Catholicism, and in Preston, as in other places, those believing in it had to conduct their services privately, and in out-of-the-way places. In Ribbleton Lane there is an old barn, still standing, wherein mass used to be said at night-time. People living in the neighbourhood fancied for a considerable period that this place was haunted; they could see a light in it periodically; they couldn't account for it; and they concluded that some headless woman or wandering gnome was holding a grim revel in it. But the fact was, a small band of Catholics debarred from open worship, and forced to secrete themselves during the hours of devotion, were gathered there.

it was pulled down by an infuriated mob

When the storm of persecution had subsided a little, Catholics in various parts of the country gradually, though quietly, got their worship into towns; and, ultimately, we find that in Preston a small thatched building —situated in Chapel Yard, off Friargate —was opened for the use of Catholics. This was in 1605. The yard, no doubt, took its name from the chapel, which was dedicated to St. Mary. There was wisdom in the selection of this spot, and appropriateness, too—it was secluded, near the heart of the town, and very close to the old thoroughfare whose very name was redolent of Catholicity. Friargate is a word which conveys its own meaning. An old writer calls it a "*fayre, long, and spacious street;*" and adds, "*upon that side of the town was formerly a large and sumptuous building belonging to the Fryers Minors or Gray Fryers, but now [1682] only reserved for the reforming of vagabonds, sturdy beggars, and petty larcenary thieves, and other people wanting good behaviour; it is now the country prison . . . and it is cal'd the House of Correction.*"

The Catholics of Preston satisfied themselves with the small building in Chapel Yard until 1761, when a new place of worship, dedicated to St. Mary, was erected upon part of the site of the convent of Grey Friars. Towards this chapel the Duke of Norfolk gave a handsome sum, and presented, for the altar, a curious painting of the Lord's Supper. But this building did not enjoy a very prosperous career, for in 1768, during a great election riot, it was pulled down by an infuriated mob, all the Catholic registers in it were burned, and the priest—the Rev. Patrick Barnewell—only saved his life by beating a rapid retreat at the rear, and crossing the Ribble at an old ford below Frenchwood. Another chapel was subsequently raised, upon the present site of St. Mary's, on the west side of Friargate, but when St. Wilfrid's was opened, in 1793, it was closed for religious purposes and transmuted into a cotton warehouse.

In 1815 the chapel was restored; but not long afterwards its roof fell in. Nobody however was hurt, just because nobody was in the building at the time. The work of reparation followed, and the chapel was deemed sufficient till 1856, when it was entirely rebuilt and enlarged. It is a chapel of ease for St. Wilfrid's, and is attended to a very large extent by Irish people.

St Mary's Catholic Chapel — People & Priest

Large congregations attend this chapel. At the rear, where many of the poor choose to sit, some of the truest specimens of the *'finest pisantry,'* some of the choicest and most aromatic Hibernians we have seen, are located. The old swallow-tailed Donnybrook Fair coat, the cutty knee-breeches, the short pipe in the waistcoat pocket, the open shirt collar, the ancient family cloak with its broad shoulder lapelle, the thick dun-coloured shawl in which many a young Patrick has been huddled up, are all visible. The elderly women have a peculiar fondness for large bonnets, decorated in front with huge borders running all round the face like frilled night-caps. The whole of the worshippers at the lower end seem a pre-eminently devotional lot. How they are at home we can't tell; but from the moment they enter the chapel and touch the holy water stoops, which somehow persist in retaining a good thick dark sediment at the bottom, to the time they walk out, the utmost earnestness prevails amongst them.

The elderly women have a peculiar fondness for large bonnets

Considering its general character, the congregation is very orderly, and we believe of a generous turn of mind. The chapel is cleanly kept by an amiable old Catholic....and there is an air of freedom and homeliness about it which we have not noticed at several places of worship.

Each Wednesday evening a service is held in the chapel, and it is most excellently attended, although some who visit it put in a rather late appearance. When we were in the chapel, one Wednesday evening, ten persons came five minutes before the service was over, and one slipped round the door side and made a descent upon the holy water forty-five seconds before the business terminated. Of course it is better late than never, only not much bliss follows late attendance, and hardly a toothful of ecstasy can be obtained in three-quarters of a minute.

During the past ten years the Rev. Thomas Brindle, of St. Wilfrid's, has been the officiating priest at St. Mary's. Father Brindle is a Fylde man, is about 45 years of age, and is a thoroughly healthy subject. He is at least 72 inches high, is well built, powerful, straight as a die, good looking, keeps his teeth clean, and attends most regularly to his clerical duties. He is unassuming in manner, blithe in company, earnest in the pulpit. His gesticulation is decisive, his lungs are good, and his vestments fit him well. Not a more stately, yet homely looking, honest-faced priest have we seen for many a day. There is nothing sinister nor subtle in his visage; the sad ferocity glancing out of some men's eyes is not seen in his. We have not yet confessed our sins to him, but we fancy he will be a kindly soul when behind the curtain, —would sooner order boiled than hard peas to be put into one's shoes by way of penance, would far rather recommend a fast on salmon than a feast on bacon, and would generally prefer a soft woollen to a hard horse hair shirt in the moments of general mortification. Father Brindle! —Give us your hand, and may you long retain a kindly regard for boiled peas, soft shirts, and salmon. They are amongst the very best things out if rightly used, and we shouldn't care about agonising the flesh with them three times a week.

St. Augustine's Catholic Church

This church is of a retiring disposition; it occupies a very southern position; is neither in the town nor out of it; and unlike many sacred edifices is more than 50 yards from either a public-house or a beershop. Clean-looking dwellings immediately confront it; green fields take up the background; an air of quietude, half pastoral, half genteel, pervades it; but this ecclesiastical rose has its thorn. Only in its proximate surroundings is the place semi-rural and select. As the circle widens—townwards at any rate—you soon get into a region of murky houses, ragged children, running beer jugs, poverty; and as you move onwards, in certain directions, the plot thickens, until you get into the very lairs of ignorance, depravity, and misery. Much honest industry, much straight-forwardness and every day kindness, much that smells of gin, and rascality, and heathenism may be seen in the district. There is plenty of room for all kinds of reformers in the locality; and if any man can do any good in it, whatever may be his creed or theory, let him do it.

There are three of those very terrible places called confessionals at St. Augustine's, and one day not so long since we visited all of them. It is enough for an ordinary sinner to patronise one confessional in a week, or a month, or a quarter of a year, and then go home and try to behave himself. But we went to three in one forenoon with a priest, afterwards had the courage to get into the very centre of a neighbouring building wherein were two and twenty nuns, and then reciprocated compliments with an amiable young lady called the *Mother Superior.*' Terrible places to enter, and most unworldly people to visit, we fancy some of our Protestant friends will say; but we saw nothing very agonising or dreadful —not even in the confessionals. Like other folk we had heard grim tales about such places—about trap doors, whips, manacles, and all sorts of cruel oddities; but in the confessionals visited we beheld nothing of any of them.

The great bulk of the congregation are calm and unostentatious, evincing a quiet demeanour in conjunction with a determined devotion. There are several very excellent sleepers in the multitude of worshippers; but they are mainly at the entrance end where they are least seen. We happened to be at the church the other Sunday morning and in **in ten minutes after the sermon began about 16 persons were fast asleep** ten minutes after the sermon began about 16 persons, all within a moderate space, were fast asleep. Their number increased slowly till the conclusion.

The average number hearing mass on a Sunday is 3,290. On four consecutive Sundays recently —from February 14 to March 14 —upwards of 13,100 heard mass within the walls of the church.

The Rev. Canon Walker is a good type of a thoroughly English priest and of a genuine Lancashire man. He is a man of peace, of homely disposition, of kindly thought, unobtrusive in style, sincere in action, with nothing bombastic in his nature, and nothing self-righteous in his speech. His sermons are neither profound nor simple —they are made up of fair medium material; and are discharged rapidly. Average talkers can get through about 120 words in a minute; Canon Walker can manage 200 nicely, and show no signs of being out of breath.

St. Joseph's Catholic Church

St. Joseph's stands on the eastern side of Preston, and is surrounded by a rapidly-developing population. The district has a South Staffordshire look —is full of children, little groceries, public-houses and beershops, brick kilns, smoke, smudge, clanging hammers, puddle-holes, dogs, cats, vagrant street hens, unmade roads, and general bewilderment.

In 1860, a Catholic school was erected in Rigby Street, Ribbleton Lane. Directly afterwards divine service was held in the building, which in its religious character was devoted to St. Joseph. But either the walls of the edifice were too weak, or the roof of it too strong, for symptoms of *'giving way'* soon set in, and the place had to be pulled down. In 1866, having been rebuilt and enlarged, it was re-opened. In the meantime, religious services and scholastic training being essential, and it being considered too far to go to St. Ignatius's and St.Augustine's, which were the places patronised prior to the opening of St. Joseph's mission, another school, with accommodation in it for divine worship, was erected on a plot of land immediately adjoining. Nearly one half of the money required for this building, which was opened in 1864, was given by Protestants.

Nearly one half of the money required ...... was given by Protestants

The half-past nine o'clock mass on a Sunday morning is a treat; for at it you can see a greater gathering of juvenile bazouks than at any other place in the town. Some of the roughest-headed lads in all creation are amongst them; their hair seems to have been allowed to have its own way from infancy, and it refuses to be dictated to now. The congregation is a very poor one, and this will be at once apparent when we state that the general income of the place, the entire proceeds of it, do not exceed £100 a year. Nearly every one attending the chapel is a factory worker, and the present depressed state of the cotton trade has consequently a special and a very crushing bearing upon the mission. A new church is badly wanted here; in no part of the town is a large place of worship so much required; but nothing can be done in the matter until the times mend. A plot of land has been secured for a church on the western side of the present improvised chapel, but until money can be found, or subscribed, or borrowed without interest, it will have to remain as at present.

Father Walmsley is a placid, studious-looking, even-tempered gentleman who has got on some distance with the work. He is thoughtful, but there is much sly humour in him; he is cautious but free when aired a little. He knows more than many would give him credit for; whilst naturally reticent and cool he is by no means dull; he is shrewd and far-seeing but calm and unassuming; and though evenly balanced in disposition be would manifest a crushing temper if roughly pulled by the ears. Father Parkinson is a native of the Fylde, and he has got much of the warm healthy blood of that district in his veins. He has a smart, gentlemanly figure; has a sharp, beaming, rubicund face; has buoyant spirits, and likes a good stiff tale; is full of life, and has an eye in his head as sharp as a hawk's; has a hot temper—a rather dignified irascible disposition; believes in sarcasm, in keen cutting hits; can scold beautifully; knows what he is about; has a *'young-man-from-the-country-but-you-don't-get-over-me'* look; is a hard worker, a careful thinker, and considers that this world as well as the next ought to be enjoyed.

St. Walburge's Catholic Church

Tradition hath it that once upon a time —about 1160 years ago —a certain West Saxon King had a daughter, whose name was Walburge; that she went into Germany with two of her brothers, became abbess of a convent there, did marvellous things, was a wonder in her way, couldn't be bitten by dogs —they used to snatch half a yard off and then run; that she died on the 25th February, 778; that her relics were transferred, on the 12th October following, to Eichstadt, at which place a convent was built to her memory; that the said relics were put into a bronze shrine, which was placed upon a table of marble, in the convent chapel; that every year since then, between the 12th of October and the 25th of February, the marble upon which the shrine is placed has 'perspired' a liquid which is collected below in a vase of silver; and that this liquid, which is called 'St. Walburge's oil,' will cure, by its application, all manner of physical ailments. This is the end of our first lesson concerning St. Walburge and the wonderful oil.

the bones immediately snapped together and she was perfectly cured

The second lesson runneth thus: About five and twenty years ago there lived, as housemaid at St. Wilfrid's presbytery, in this town, one Alice Holderness. She was a comely woman and pious; but she fell one day on some steps leading to the presbytery, hurt one of her legs—broke the knee cap of it, we believe—and had to be carried straight to bed. Medical aid was obtained; but the injured knee was obstinate, wouldn't be mended, and when physic and hope alike had been abandoned, so far as the leg of Alice was concerned, the Rev. Father Norris, who, in conjunction with the Rev. Father Weston, was at that time stationed at St. Wilfrid's, was struck with a somewhat bright thought as to the potency of St. Walburge's oil. A little of that oil was procured, and this is what a sister of the injured woman says, in a letter which we have seen on the subject, viz.: That Father Norris dipped a pen into the oil and dropped a morsel of it upon her knee, whereupon *"the bones immediately snapped together and she was perfectly cured, having no longer the slightest weakness in the broken limb."*

This is a strange tale, which people can either believe or disbelieve at their own pleasure. All Protestants —ourselves included —will necessarily be dubious; and if any polemical lecturer should happen to see the story he will go wild with delight, and consider that there is material enough in it for at least six good declamatory and paying discourses.

Well, whether correct or false, the priests at St. Wilfrid's believed in the 'miraculous cure,' and decided forthwith to agitate for a church in honour of St. Walburge.

That church is the one we now see on Maudlands—a vast and magnificent pile, larger in its proportions than any other Preston place of worship, and with a spire which can only be equalled for altitude by two others in the whole country. What a potent architectural charm was secreted in that mystic oil with which Father Norris touched the knee of Alice! In the 'Walpurgis dance of globule and oblate spheroid,' there may be something wonderful, but through this drop of oil from the Walpurgian shrine an obstreperous knee snapped up into compact health instantly, and then a large church, ornamental to Preston and creditable to the entire Catholic population, arose.

St. Walburge's — its Spire & its People

The most prominent thing about the church is the spire, which, as well as the tower, is built of limestone, and surmounted by a cross, the distance from its apex to the ground being about 301 feet. We saw the weather vane fixed upon this spire, and how the man who did the job managed to keep his head from spinning right round, and then right off, was at the time an exciting mystery to us which we have not yet been able to properly solve. A little before the actual completion of the spire, we had a chance of ascending it, but we remained below. The man in charge wanted half-a-crown for the trip; and as we fancied that something like £5 ought to be given to us for undertaking a journey so perilous, it was mutually decided that we should keep down. Why, it would be a sort of agony to ascend the spire under the most favourable circumstances; and as one might only tumble down if ascension were achieved, the safest plan is to keep down altogether. We have often philosophised on the question of punishment, and, locally speaking, we have come to this conclusion, that agony would be sufficiently piled in any case of crime, if the delinquent were just hoisted to the top of St. Walburge's spire and left there. From the summit of the tower, which is quite as high as safe-sided human beings need desire to get, there is a magnificent view: Preston lurches beneath like a hazy amphitheatre of houses and chimneys; to the east you have Pendle, Longridge, and the dark hills of Bowland; northwards, in the far distance, the undulating Lake hills; westward, the fertile Fylde, flanked by the Ribble, winding its way like a silver thread to the ocean; and southwards Rivington Pyke and Hoghton's wooded summit with a dim valley to the left thereof, in which Blackburn works and dreams out its vigorous existence. The general scenery from the tower is panoramic and charming. The view from the spire head must be immense and exquisite, but few people of this generation, unless a very safe plan of ascension is found out, will be able to enjoy it.

The worshippers at this church are, in nine cases out of ten, working people. The better class of people sit at the higher end of the central benches; and if one had never seen them there no difficulty would be experienced in finding out their seats. You may always ascertain the character of worshippers by what they sit upon. Working-class people rest upon bare boards; middle-class individuals develop the cushion scheme to a moderate pitch; the upper species push it towards consummation-like ease, and therefore are the owners of good cushions. Very few cushions can be seen in St. Walburge's; those noticeable are at the higher end; and the logical inference, therefore, is that not many superb people attend the place, and that those who do go sit just in the quarter mentioned.

Father Papall has a sweeping powerful voice; you could almost hear him if you were asleep, and this fact may account for the peculiarly contented movements of several parties we observed recently at the church whilst he was preaching. At least 20 near us went to sleep in about five minutes after he began talking, slept very well during the whole sermon, and at its conclusion woke up very refreshed, made brisk crosses, listened awhile to the succeeding music, &c., and then walked out quite cool and cheerful.

The Wesleyan Methodists

Wesleyan Methodism first breathed and opened its eyes in or about the year 1729. It was nursed in its infancy at Oxford by two rare brothers and a few students; was christened at the same place by a keenly-observing, slightly-satirical collegian; developed itself gradually through the country; took charge of the neglected masses and gave them a new life; and today it is one of the great religious forces of the world.

The orthodox looked down with a genteel contempt upon the preachers whose religion had converted Kingswood colliers, and turned Cornwall wreckers into honest men; and the formally pious spoke of the worshippers at this new shrine of faith with a serene sneer, and classed them as a parcel of fiercely ejaculating, hymn-singing nonentities. But there was vitality at the core of their creed, and its fuller triumphs were but a question of time.

In 1817, Methodism became dissatisfied with its first quarters in Back Lane, and migrated into a lighter, healthier, and cleaner portion of the town —Lune Street—where a building was erected for its special convenience and edification. It was not a very elegant structure; it was, in fact, a plain, phlegmatic aggregation of brick and mortar, calculated to charm no body externally, and evidently patronised for absolute internal rapture. In 1861 the chapel was rebuilt —enlarged, beautified, and made fine, so as to harmonise with the laws of modern fashion, and afford easy sitting room for the large and increasing congregation attending it. The frontispiece is of a costly character; but it has really been *'born to blush unseen.'* It is so tightly wedged in between other buildings, is so evenly crammed into companionship with the ordinary masonry of the street, that the general effect of the tall arch and spacious porch is lost. Nothing can be distinctly seen at even a moderate distance. You have to get to the place before you become clearly aware of its existence; and if you wish to know anything of its appearance, you have either to turn the head violently off its regular axis, or cross the street and ask somebody for a step ladder.

There is something humorous and incongruous in the physical associations of this chapel. It is flanked with a doctor's shop and a money-lending establishment; with a savings bank and a solicitor's office. The bank nestles very complacently under its lower wing, and in the ratio of its size is a much better looking building. The text regarding the deposit of treasure in that place where neither moth nor rust operate may be well worked in the chapel; but it is rather at a discount in the immediate neighbourhood.

A great work in the business of spreading Wesleyan Methodism has been done by the people and parsons of Lune Street chapel. We know of no place in the town whose religious influence has been more actively radiated. Its power, a few years ago, spread into the northern part of the town, and the result was a new chapel with excellent schools there; it then moved eastward, and the consequence was a school chapel in St. Mary Street. In Croft Street, Canal Street, and on the Marsh, it has also outposts, whose officers are fighting the good fight with lung, and head, and heart, in a sprightly and vigorous fashion.

> **fighting the good fight with lung, and head, and heart**

Lune Street Methodist Chapel

This is the fashionable Wesleyan tabernacle of Preston; the better end of those whose minds have been touched, through either tradition or actual conviction, with the beauties of Methodism, frequent it. In the congregation there are many most excellent, hardworking, thoroughly sincere men and women, who would be both useful and ornamental to any body of Christians under the sun; but there are in addition, as there are in every building set apart for the purposes of piety, several who have '*more frill than shirt*' and much '*more cry than wool*' about them—rectified, beautifully self-righteous, children who would '*sugar over*' a very ugly personage ten hours out of the twelve every day, and then at night thank the Lord for all his mercies.

In Lune Street Chapel faction used to run high and wilfulness was a gem which many of the members wore very near their hearts; but much of the old feudal spirit of party fighting has died out, and there are signs of pious resignation and loving kindness in the flock, which would at one time have been rare jewels. A somewhat lofty isolation is still manifested here and there; a few regular attenders appear heavily oppressed with the idea that they are not only as good as anybody else but much better. Still this is only human nature and no process of convertibility to the most celestial of substances can in this world entirely subdue it. The bruising deacon who said that grace was a good thing, but that knocking down an impertinent member was better, didn't miss the bull's eye of natural philosophy very far. The observation was not redolent of much Christian spirit; but it evinced that which many of the saints are troubled with—human nature.

The singing is neither loftily classic nor contemptibly common-place. It is good, medium, well modulated melody, heartily got up; and thoroughly congregational. In some places of worship it is considered somewhat vulgar for members of the congregation to give specimens of their vocalisation; and you can only find in out-of-the-way side and back pews odd persons warbling a mild falsetto, or piping an eccentric tenor, or doing a heavy bass on their own responsibility; but at Lune Street Chapel the general members of the congregation go into the work with a distinct determination to either sing or make a righteous noise worthy of the occasion.

The more genteel worshippers take up their quarters mainly on the ground floor—at the back of the central seats and at the sides. The poor have resting places found for them immediately in front of the pulpit and at the rear of the galleries. Very little of that unctuous spasmodic shouting, which used to characterise Wesleyanism, is heard in Lune Street Chapel. It has become unfashionable to bellow; it is not considered '*the thing*' to ride the high horse of vehement approval and burst into luminous showers of '*Amens*' and '*Halleleujahs.*' Now and then a few worshippers of the ancient type drop in from some country place, and explode at intervals during the course of some impulsive prayer, or gleeful hymn, or highly enamelled sermon. You may occasionally at such a time, hear two or three in distant pews having a delightful time of it. But hardy a scintilla of this is perceived on ordinary occasions; indeed it has become so unpopular that an exhibition of it seems to quietly amuse—to evoke mild smiles and dubious glances—rather than meet with reciprocity of approval.

> It has become unfashionable to bellow

29

The Primitive Methodists

There is nothing very time-worn about Methodism; it is only 140 years old; but during that period its admirers have contrived to split numerous hairs, and have extended very fairly what is known as '*the dissidence of dissent*.' The ring of Methodism includes many sections: it embraces, amongst others, ordinary Wesleyans, Bryanites, New Connectionists, Primitives, United Free Church men, and Independent Methodists. They can't all be right; but they think they are; and that is enough. They have as yet requested nobody to be responsible for them; and weighing that over well, the fairest plan is to let the creed of each alone —to condemn none, to give all legitimate chance, and permit them to '*go on.*' Antique simplicity seems to be the virtue of those whom we have now to describe. And yet there is nothing very ancient about them. There is more in the sound than in the name of Primitive Methodists. They are a comparatively young people with a somewhat venerable name.

it was quite enough to hear women talk at home

Originally they were connected with the Wesleyan Methodists; but they disagreed with them in the course of time, and left them eventually. The immediate cause of separation was, we are informed, a dispute as to the propriety of camp meetings, and the utility of female preaching. The Wesleyans couldn't see the wisdom of such meetings nor the fun of such preaching: probably they thought that people could get as much good as they would reasonably digest in regular chapel gatherings, and that it was quite enough to hear women talk at home without extending the business to pulpits. The Primitives believed otherwise—fancied that camp meetings would be productive of much Christian blissfulness, and thought that females had as much right to give pulpit as Caudle* lectures. With a chivalry nearly knightly they came to the rescue, and gave woman a free pass into the regions of language and theology. Primitive Methodism does not profess to be a fine, but an earnest, thing—not a trimmed-up, lackadaisical arrangement, but a strong, sincere, simple, enthusiastic species of religion. It has largely to do with the heart and the feelings; is warm-natured, full of strong, straightforward, devotional vigour; combines homeliness of soul with intensity of imagination; links a great dash of honest turbulence with an infinitude of deep earnestness; tells a man that if he is happy he may shout, that if under a shower of grace he may fly off at a tangent and sing; makes a sinner wince awfully when under the pang of repentance, and orders him to jump right out of his skin for joy the moment he finds peace; gives him a fierce cathartic during conversion, and a rapturous cataplasm in his '*reconciliation*.' Primitive Methodism occupies the same place in religion as the ballad does in poetry. It has an untamed, blithesome, healthy ring with it; harmonises well with the common instincts and the broad, common intuitions of common life; can't hurt a prince, and will improve a peasant; won't teach a king wrong things; is sure to infuse happiness amongst men of humbler mould.

We have a considerable regard for Primitive Methodism; in some respects we admire its operations; and for the good it does we are quite willing to tolerate all the erratic earnestness, musical effervescence, and prayerful boisterousness it is so enamoured of. Primitive Methodism has reached deeper depths than many other creeds —has touched harder, wilder, ruder souls than nearly '*all the isms*' put together.

*Writer D W Jerrold (1803-1857) created a comic series entitled 'Mrs Caudle's Curtain Lectures' for Punch magazine. The lectures were supposedly given by Mrs Caudle to her husband as they lay together in bed, the only time she could talk to him without interruption.

Preston's Primitive Methodists

The first regular quarters of Preston Primitive Methodism were in Friargate, in a yard facing Lune Street —in a small building there, where a few men with strong lungs and earnest minds had many seasons of rejoicing. The thermometer afterwards rose; and for some time a building which they erected in Lawson Street, and which is now used as the Weavers' Institute, was occupied by them. Often did they get far up the dreamy ladder of religious joy, and many a time did they revel with a rich and deafening delightfulness in the regions of zeal there. They were determined to 'keep the thing warm,' and to let outsiders know that if they were not a large, they were a lively, body.

In 1836 the Primitive Methodists left their Lawson Street seminary and pitched their tent eastwards —on a piece of land facing Saul Street and flanking Lamb Street. Its situation is pretty good, and as it stands right opposite, only about eight yards from, the Baths and Washhouses, we would suggest to the Saul Street brethren the propriety of putting up some sign, or getting some inscription made in front of their chapel, to the effect that 'cleanliness is next to godliness,' and that both can be obtained on easy terms.

There are about 400 members in connection with the place, and they respectively contribute 1d. per week towards the expenses. The congregation is almost entirely of a working-class character. In the front and on each side of the body of the building there are a few free seats, which are mainly used by very poor humble-looking people.

The singing is thoroughly congregational —permeates the whole place, is shot out in a quick, cheerful strain, is always strong and merry, is periodically excellent, is often jolly and funny, has sometimes a sort of chorus to

the singing is a simple process of pious refreshment and exhileration

it, and altogether is a strong, virtuously-jocund, free and easy piece of ecstasy which the people enjoy much. It would stagger a man fond of 'linked sweetness long drawn out,' it might superinduce a mortal ague in one too enamoured of Handel and Mozart; but to those who regularly attend the place, who have got fairly upon the lines of Primitive action, it is a simple process of pious refreshment and exhilaration.

The ministers are paid on a systematic and considerate plan. Money is given to them to accordance with the number of their family. They get so much per head —the more numerous the family and the larger the pay becomes. But it is not very extraordinary at the best of times; and if even a preacher happened to have a complete houseful of children, if his quiver were absolutely full of them, he would not be pecuniarly rich. The bulk of Primitive Methodist preachers are taken from the working classes, and the pay they receive is not more than they could earn if they kept out of the ministry altogether. They become parsons for the love of 'the cause,' and not for loaves and fishes.

There are numerous collections, some fixed, and some incidental, at Saul Street, and on special occasions they can raise sums of money which would put to the blush the bulk of loftier and more 'respectable' congregations. Their prayer meetings are pious and gleeful affairs. Throughout the whole of such gatherings, and in fact generally when prayer is being gone on with, the steam is kept well up, and the safety valve often lifts to let off the extra pressure. Sharp shouts, breezy 'Amens,' tenderly-attenuated groans, deep sighs, sudden 'Hallelujahs,' and vivacious cries of 'Just now,' 'Aye,' 'Glory,' 'Yes,' 'Praise the Lord,' &c.—all well meant–characterise them.

United Methodist Free Church

This chapel is the successor, in a direct line, of the first building ever erected in the Orchard. Its ancestor was placed on precisely the same spot, in 1831. Those who raised it seceded from the Wesleyan community, in sympathy with the individuals who retired from the *'old body'* at Leeds, in 1828, and who adopted the name of *'Protestant Methodists.'* For a short time the Preston branch of these Methodists worshipped in that mystic nursery of germinating *'isms'* called Vauxhall Road Chapel; and in the year named they erected in the Orchard a building for their own spiritual improvement. It was a plain chapel outside, and mortally ugly within. Amongst the preaching confraternity in the connexion it used to be known as *'the ugliest Chapel in Great Britain and Ireland.'* In 1834 a further secession of upwards of 20,000 from the Wesleyans took place, under the leadership of the late Dr. Warren, of Manchester. These secessionists called themselves the *'Wesleyan Association,'* and with them the *'Protestant Methodists,'* including those meeting in the Orchard Chapel, Preston, amalgamated. They also adopted the name of their new companions. In 1857 the *'Wesleyan Association'* coalesced with another large body of persons, who seceded from the original Wesleyans in 1849, under the leadership of the Rev. James Everett and others, and the two conjoined sections termed themselves the *'United Methodist Free Church.'* None of the separations recorded were occasioned by any theological difference with the parent society, but through disagreement on matters of *'government.'*

The *'members'* support their churches, financially, in accordance with their means. There is no fixed payment. Those who are better off, and not stingy, give liberally; the less opulent contribute moderately; those who can't give anything don't. After an existence of about 30 years, the old chapel in the Orchard was pulled down, in order to make way for a larger and a better looking building. During the work of reconstruction Sunday services were held in the school at the rear, which was built some time before, at a cost of £1,700. The new chapel, which cost £2,600, was opened on the 22nd of May, 1862. It has a rather ornamental front —looks piquant and seriously nobby. There is nothing of the *'great'* or the *'grand'* in any part of it. The building is diminutive, cheerful, well-made, and inclined, in its stone work, to be fantastical.

The present minister of the chapel is the Rev. Richard Abercrombie. He is an elderly gentleman —must be getting near 70; but he is almost as straight as a wand, has a dignified look, wears a venerable grey beard, and has quite a military precision in his form and walk. And he may well have, for he has been a soldier; Mr. Abercrombie served in the British army upwards of twenty years. He followed Wellington after Waterloo, and was in Paris as a British soldier when the famous treaty of peace was signed. His grandfather was cousin of the celebrated Sir Ralph Abercrombie, who defeated Napoleon's forces in Egypt, and his ancestors held commissions in our army for upwards of four generations. Tired of military life, Mr. Abercrombie eventually laid down his arms, and for 33 years he has been a minister in the body he is now connected with. He has two or three sons in the United Methodist Free Church ministry, and one of them, called after the general who defeated the Napoleonic forces, is the only man belonging the body who has a university M.A. after his name.

the ugliest Chapel in Great Britain and Ireland

Croft Street Wesleyan Methodists

We sat down near a young gentleman with a strong bass voice. In a corner near there was a roseate-featured, elderly man, who enjoyed the service at intervals and slept out what he could not fathom. Close to him was a youth who did the very same thing; and in front there were three females who followed the like example. The service was plain, simple, sincere, and quite Methodistical; nothing approaching either cant or wild-fire was manifested. Working-class people preponderated in the place, as they always do; the singing was clear, and plain, odd lines coming in for a share of melodious quavering; and the sermon was well got-up and eloquent. The Rev. C. F. Hame is a little gentleman, with considerable penetration and power; has a good theological faculty; is cool, genial, and lucid in language; and, although he can shout a little when very warm, he never loses either the thread of his argument or his personal equilibrium.

Such a noise as this...ought to have aroused the whole neighbourhood

Regular ministers and local preachers fill the pulpit in turns; there being, as a rule, one of the former at either the morning or evening service every Sunday. Sometimes both kinds may be present and ready for action at the same moment; but they never quarrel as to which shall preach —never get '*up a tree,*' figuratively speaking, and everything is arranged quietly. The school, wherein the services we have referred to are held, has been one of the most useful in Preston; more scholars have probably passed through it than through any other similar place in the town; old scholars—men and women now—who received their religious education here, are in all parts, and there is not a quarter of the globe where some may not be found who have a pleasant recollection of the school.

Parker Street United Methodist Free Church

There was a dispute amongst the United Free Church brethren assembling in Orchard Chapel. Both men and women entered into the disturbance freely; but they did not follow the plan lately adopted by some United Methodist Christians, living at Batley, who, having a grievance at their chapel, '*fought it out*' in the back yard; what they did, after many a lively church meeting, was to appeal to the authorities of the denomination, state their case quietly, and abide the decision of their superiors. That decision sanctioned a separation and the establishment in Preston of a second United Methodist circuit, totally independent of the Orchard Street people.

Several yards before we reached the building, the torrents of a strong voice came impetuously through an open window, and the burthen of its strains had reference to a revival of '*our connexion.*' Such a noise as this we thought ought to have aroused the whole neighbourhood; but we could see nobody about except a woman right opposite, who was engaged in the serious business of front step washing, and who seemed to take no notice whatever of the strong utterances coming through the window. She washed on, and the good man above prayed on. We were surprised at the cleanness and neatness of the building, and at the large number of people within it. Rumour had conveyed to us a notion that about three persons visited this chapel; but we found between 100 and 200—all well-dressed, orderly, and pleasant—in attendance. We also noticed a policeman amongst the company. He was present, not to keep the peace, but to get some good, for Heaven knows that policemen need much of the article, and that they have very little Sunday time to find it in. The policeman behaved himself very well during the whole service.

Wesley Chapel in North Road

People have a particular liking for whoever or whatever may be called after them, and good old John may sometimes look down approvingly upon the place and tell Charles that he likes it. The chapel, built in 1838, enjoys the usual society of all pious buildings: it has two public houses and a beer shop within thirty yards of its entrance, and they often seem to be doing a brisker business than it can drive, except during portions of the Sunday when they are shut up, and, consequently, have not a fair chance of competing with it.

The average attendance will be about 800; and nearly every one making up that number belongs to the working-class section of life. Amongst the body are many genial good-hearted folk-people who believe in doing right without telling everybody about it, in obliging you without pulling a face over it; and there are also individuals in the rank and file of worshippers who are very Pecksniffian and dismal, cranky, windy, authoritative, who would look sour if eating sugar, would call a 'church meeting' if you wore a lively suit of clothes, and would tell you that they were entitled to more grace than anybody else, and had got more.

Worship is conducted in the chapel with considerable quietness. You may hear the long-drawn gelatinous sigh, the subdued, quiet, unctuous 'amen,' and if the thing gets hot a few lively half-innate exclamations are thrown into the proceedings. But there is nothing in any of them of a turbulent or riotous character. The parsons can draw out none of the worshippers into a very ungovernable frame of mind; and we believe none of the people have for some time been very violent in either their verbal expressions or physical contortions. They are beginning to take things quietly, and to work inwardly during periods of bliss.

Moor Park Wesleyan Chapel

The Rev. T. A. Rayner is an elderly gentleman, with a strong osseous frame, which is well covered with muscle and adipose matter; he has been about 34 years in the ministry, and should, therefore, be either very smart or very dull by this time. He has a portly, grave, reverential look; carries with him both spectacles and an eye-glass; is slow and coldly-keen in his mental processes; thinks that he can speak with authority; and that all minor dogs must cease barking when he mounts the oracular tripod; he is sincere; works well, for his years, and in his own way does his best.

He has many good properties; but short sermon preaching is not one of them; he can, like the east wind, blow a long while in one direction. One Sunday evening, when we heard him, be preached just one hour, and at the conclusion intimated that he had been requested to give a short sermon, but had drifted into a rather prolix one. We should like to know what length he would have run out his rhetoric if he had been requested to give a long discourse. By the powers! it would have 'tickled the catastrophe' of each listener finely—doctors would have had to be called in, a vast amount of physic would have been required, and it would never have got paid for in these hard times so that bad debts would have been added to the general calamity. We could never see any good in long sermons and nobody else ever could except those giving them. Neither could we ever see much fun in a parson saying—'And now lastly' more than once. In the 60 minutes discourse to which we have alluded, the preacher got into the lastly part of the business five times. If that other conclusive phrase—'And now, finally brethren'—had been taken advantage of, and similarly worked, we might never have got home till morning.

Lancaster Road Congregational Chapel

Preston Congregationalism is a very good, a very respectable, and a very quarrelsome creature. It is liberal but gingerly; has a large regard for freedom, but will quarrel if crossed; can achieve commendable triumphs in the regions of peace, but likes a conscientious disturbance at intervals; believes in the power of union, but acts as if a split were occasionally essential; will nurse its own children well when they are quiet, but recognises the virtues of a shake if uneasiness supervenes; respects its ministers much, but will order them to move on if they fret its epidermis too acutely; can pray well, work well, fight well; and from its antagonisms can distil benefits. About nine years since, a sacred stirring of heads, a sharp moving of tongues, and a lively up-heaving of bristles took place at Cannon Street Congregational Chapel, in this town. The result of the dispute involved, amongst other things, a separation—a clear marching from the place of several parties who, whether rightly or wrongly, matters not now, felt themselves aggrieved. They did not leave the chapel in processional order, neither did they throw stones and then run, when they took their departure. The process of evaporation was quiet and orderly. For 12 months the seceders worshipped on their own account, and negotiated for land upon which to build a new chapel and schools; and finally they purchased a site on the higher side of the Orchard, contiguous to the old Vicarage—a rare piece of antique, rubbishy ruin in these days—and very near, if not actually upon, ground which once formed the garden of the famous Isaac Ambrose, who was Vicar of Preston in 1650, and afterwards ejected, with many more in the land, on account of his religious opinions. Thinking it good to harmonise with that ancient wisdom which recommends people to carry the calf before beginning with the cow, the new band of Congregationalists under notice, commenced operations on the site named by erecting a large school room in which for about a year they worshipped. In due time they got the chapel built, and for about seven years it has been open.

The pews in the chapel are very strong, have receding backs, and make sitting in them rather a pleasing, easy, contented affair. The highest price for a single seat is 3s. 6d. per quarter; the lowest 1s. There are a few free sittings in the place, and although they may seem a long way back—being at the rear of the gallery—their position is not to be despised. They are not so far distant as to render hearing difficult; and they obviate that unseemly publicity which is given to poor people in some places of worship. How to give the poorest and hungriest folk a very good seat in a very prominent place—how to herd them together and piously pen them up in some particular place where everybody can see them—appears to be an object in many religious edifices. But that is a piece of benevolent shabbiness which must come to grief some day. In the meantime, and until the period arrives when honest poverty will be considered no crime, and when a seat next to a poor man will be thought nothing vulgar, or contaminating, whilst worshipping before Him who cares for souls not lucre, hearts not wealth, let the poor be put in some place where they can hear fairly without being unduly exhibited.

> *Let the poor be put in some place where they can hear fairly without being unduly exhibited*

35

Fishergate Baptist Chapel

In Preston, as elsewhere, the majority of people think well of water when it is required by children for engulfing or baptismal purposes; but they care little for its use when the teens have been trotted through. It may be right enough for the physical and religious comfort of babes and sucklings; but its virtues recede in the ratio of development. There are, however, some sections of men and women in the town who, symbolically at least, have a high regard for water at any time after the years of sense and reason have been reached. These are the Baptists. There are four or five chapels set apart for their improvement in Preston, and the smartest of these is in Fishergate.

What Lune Street is to the Wesleyans, so Fishergate seems to be to the Baptists—the centre of gravity of the more refined and fashionable worshippers. Very few poor people visit it, and it is thought that if they don't come of their own accord they will never be seriously pressed on the subject. The congregation consists almost entirely of middle-class persons—people who have either saved money in business or who are making a determined effort to do so. Nothing approaching fervour ever takes possession of the general body. Religion with them is not a termagant, revered for her sauciness and loved for her violent evolutions. It is a reticent, even spirited, calmly orthodox affair, whose forerunner fed on locusts and wild honey, and whose principles are to be digested quietly. There may be a few very boisterous sheep in the fold, who get on fire periodically in the warmth of speaking and praying; who will express their willingness, when the pressure is up, to do any mortal thing for the good of 'the cause;' but who will have to be caught there and then if anything substantial has to follow. Like buckwheat cakes and rum gruel they are

Nothing approaching fervour ever takes possession of the general body

best whilst hot.

The baptistery in Fishergate Chapel is used two or three times a year, and if outsiders happen to get a whisper of an intended dipping, curiosity leads them to the chapel, and they look upon the ceremony as a piece of sacred fun, right enough to look at, but far too wet for anything else. This dipping is, indeed, a quaint, cold piece of business. None except adults or youths who have, it is thought, come to sense and reason, are permitted to pass through the ordeal, and it is recognised by them as symbolic of their entrance into 'the Church.' Sometimes as many as six or seven are immersed. They put on old or special garments suitable for the occasion, and the work of baptism is then carried on by the minister, who stands in the figurative Jordan. He quietly ducks them overhead; they submit to the process without a murmur; they neither bubble, nor scream, nor squirm; and the elders look on solemnly, though impressed with thoughts that, excellent as the ceremony may be, it is a rather shivering sort of business after all. After being baptised, the new members retire into an adjoining room, strip their saturated cloths, rub themselves briskly with towels, or get the deacons to do the work for them, then re-dress, comb their hair, and receive liberty to rejoice with the general Israel of the flock. Such baptism as that we have described seems a rather curious kind of rite; but it is honestly believed in, and as those who submit to it have to undergo the greatest punishment in the case—have to be put right overhead in cold Longridge water—other persons may keep tolerably cool on the subject. If three-fourths of the people who now laugh at adult baptism would undergo a dipping next Sunday, and then stick to water for the remainder of their lives, they would be better citizens, whatever might become of their theology.

Grimshaw Street Independent Chapel

Long ago there was a rather curious difficulty at the Unitarian Chapel in this town. In 1807, the Rev. W. Manning Walker, who at that time had been minister of the chapel for five years, changed his mind, became '*more evangelical*,' could not agree with the doctrines he had previously preached, got into water somewhat warm with the members, and left the place. He took with him a few sympathisers, and through their instrumentality a new chapel was built for him in Grimshaw Street, and opened on the 12th of April, 1808. It was a small edifice, would accommodate about 350 persons, and was the original ancestor of the Independent Chapel in that street. In 1817 the building was enlarged so as to accommodate between 500 and 600, and Mr. Walker laboured regularly at it till 1822, when declining health necessitated his retirement. The Rev. Thomas McConnell, a gentleman with a smart polemical tongue, succeeded him. He drew large congregations, and for a time was a burning and a shining light; but in 1825 he withdrew; became an infidel or something of the sort, and subsequently gave lectures on theological subjects, much to the regret of his friends and the horror of the orthodox.

On the 23rd of July, 1826, the Rev. R. Slate began duty as regular minister, and remained until April 7th, 1861, when through old age and growing infirmity he resigned. Mr. Slate was a tiny, careful, smoothly-earnest man, consistent and faithful as a minister, made more for quiet sincere work than dashing labour or dazzling performance; fond of the Puritan divines, a believer in old manuscripts, disposed to tell his audiences every time he got upon a platform how long he had been in the ministry, but in the aggregate well and deservedly respected. No clergyman in Preston has ever stayed so long at one place as Mr. Slate; and since it lost him the chapel has many a time had a '*slate off*' in more respects than one.

After Mr. Slate retired, the Rev. J. Briggs, a young and vociferous gentleman, fresh from college, given to Sunday evening lecturing, Corn Exchange serenading, virtuous speech-making, and other—we were going to say evils—labours of love, appeared upon the stage. Soon after he arrived a new black gown was presented to him, and if one of the local papers which recorded the event at the time tells the truth, he had it donned in the vestry, after which there was a procession round the church, Mr. Briggs leading the way, whilst the deacons and others brought up the rear. If the town's beadle and mace-bearer had been present, the procession would have been complete.

In October, 1866, Mr. Briggs retired, with the gown, and he has since gone over to '*mother church*.' Before he went there were many storms at the place. The parson never got to literal fighting with any of the members; the members never threatened to hit him; but one or more of them have been heard to say that they would put him '*behind the fire*' in the vestry, and he in turn has been heard to remark that he would return the compliment. But all this sort of Christian courtesy has disappeared, let us hope forever; and the members now nestle in their seats lovingly, casting calm glances at each other betimes, and attending duly to the parson, who eyes them placidly, and encourages their affection.

> No clergyman in Preston has ever stayed so long at one place as Mr. Slate

Vauxhall Road Particular Baptist Chapel

'Don't be so particular' is a particularly popular phrase. It comes up constantly from the rough quarry of human nature—is a part of life's untamed protest against punctiliousness and mathematical virtue. Particular people are never very popular people, just because they are particular. The world isn't sufficiently ripe for niceties; it likes a lot, and pouts at eclectical squeamishness; it believes in a big, vigorous, rough-hewn medley, is choice in some of its items, but free and easy in the bulk; and it can't masticate anything too severely didactic, too purely logical, too strongly distinct, or too acutely exact. But it does not follow, etymologically, that a man is right because he is particular. He may be very good or very bad, and yet be only such because he is particularly so. Singularity, eccentricity, speciality, isolation, oddity, and hundreds of other things which might be mentioned, all involve particularity. The particular enters into all sorts of things, and it has even a local habitation and a name in religion. What could be more particular than Particular Baptism? The Particular Baptists trace their origin to a coterie of men and women who had an idea that their grace was of a special type, and who met in London as far back as 1616. The doctrines of the Particular Baptists are of the Calvinistic hue. They believe in eternal election, free justification, ultimate glorification; they have a firm notion that they are a special people, known before all time; that not one of them will be lost.

About 1848, a plain, homely, broad-hearted *'Lancashire chap,'* named Thomas Haworth, a block printer by trade, and living in the neighbourhood of Accrington, who had taken to preaching in his spare time, was *'invited'* to supply the Vauxhall Road pulpit. *'Tommy'* — that's his

> it does not follow...that a man is right because he is particular

recognized name, and he'll not be offended at us for using it—came, saw, and conquered. He made his appearance in a plain coat, a plain waist-coat, and a pair of plain blue-coloured corduroy trousers; and as he went up the steps of the pulpit, people not only wondered where he came from, but who his tailor was. And if they had seen his hat, they would have been solicitous as to its manufacturer. The more elaborate portion of the *'church'* pulled uncongenial features at the young block-printer's appearance, thought him too rough, too unreclaimed, too outspoken, and too vehement; the plain people, the humble, hard-working, unfashionable folk liked him, and said he was *'just the man'* for them. Time kept moving, Tommy was asked to officiate in the pulpit for 52 Sundays; he consented; kept up his fire well; and when settling day came a majority of the members decided that he should remain with them. The *'non-contents'* moved off, said that it would not do; was too much of a good thing; escaped to Zoar; and, in the course of this retreat, somebody took—what!—not the pulpit, nor its Bible, nor the hymn books, nor the collecting boxes, nor the unpaid bills belonging the chapel, but—the title deeds of the old place! and to this day they have not been returned.

Between 500 and 600 persons might be accommodated in the chapel; but the average attendance is below 200. People are not *'particular'* about what church or chapel they belong to in its locality; and some of them who belong to no place seem most wickedly comfortable. There is a great deal of heathenish contentment in Vauxhall Road district, and how to make the people living there feel properly miserable until they get into a Christian groove of thought is a mystery which we leave for the solution of parsons.

Zoar Particular Baptist Chapel

A stiff quarrel is about the surest and quickest thing we are acquainted with for multiplying places of worship, for Dissenters, at any rate; and probably it would be found to work with efficacy, if tried, amongst other bodies. Local experience shows that disputes in congregations invariably end in the erection of new chapels. Show us a body of hard, fiercely-quarrelsome religious people, and although neither a prophet nor the son of one we dare predict that a new place of worship will be the upshot of their contentions. We know of four or five chapels in Preston which here been raised on this plan, and those requiring more need only keep the scheme warm. It is not essential that persons anxious for new sacred edifices should expend their forces in pecuniary solicitations; let them set a few congregations by the ears and the job will be done at once.

the nursery of two or three stirring young bodies given to spiritual peculiarity

There was a small feud in 1849-50 at Vauxhall Road Particular Baptist Chapel, Preston, concerning a preacher; several liked him; some didn't; a brisk contention followed; and, in the end, the dissatisfied ones—about 50 in number, including 29 members—finding that they had '*got up a tree*,' quietly retired. They hired a place in Cannon Street, which somehow has been the nursery of two or three stirring young bodies given to spiritual peculiarity. Here they worshipped earnestly, looking out in the meantime for a plot of land in some part of the town whereon they could build a chapel, and thus attend to their own business on their own premises. This was a little spot on the north-eastern side of Regent Street, abutting upon Winckley Square. Upon this land they raised a small chapel, and dedicated it to Zoar. The chapel was opened in 1853, at a cost of £500, one-fifth of which, apart from previous subscriptions, was raised during the inaugural services.

Nearly all who visit the chapel are middle-class people. The average attendance ranges from 70 to 80. There are 34 members at the place. Half of those who originally joined it are dead. They did not die through attending the chapel, but through ordinary physical ailment. Their pulpit is specially reserved for men after their own heart. They will admit to it neither General Baptists, nor Methodists, nor Independents; and however good a thing any of the preachers of these bodies might have to say, they would have to burst before the Zoar Chapel brethren would find them rostrum accommodation for its expression. All classes, they fancy, ought to mind their own affairs; and preachers they consider should always keep to the pulpits of their own faith.

There is a debt of £150 upon Zoar Chapel; and if any gentleman will give that sum to square up matters we can guarantee that good special sermons, eulogistic of all his virtues since birth, will be preached, and that a monument will be erected to him in the chapel when he dies.

During a forenoon service the person in the pulpit was, we learned, a Fylde farmer; but he must at some time have lived in the north, for he said '*dowter*' for daughter, '*gert*' for great, '*nather*' for neither, '*natteral*' for natural, and gave his '*r's*' capital good exercise, turning them round well, throughout his entire discourse; and he cared very little for either singular or plural verbs. If he got the sense out he deemed it sufficient.

Pole Street Baptist Chapel

About 45 years ago, a small parcel of Preston people, enamoured of the Calvinistic Methodism which the Countess of Huntingdon recognised, worshipped in a building in Cannon Street. In 1825 they built, or had raised for them, a chapel in Pole Street, which was dedicated to St. Mark. At this time, probably on account of its novelty, the creed drew many followers—the new chapel was patronised by a somewhat numerous congregation, which kept increasing for a period. But it gradually dwindled down, and a total collapse finally ensued. In 1855 a number of General Baptists, who split from their brethren worshipping in the old Leeming Street chapel, struck a bargain for the building in Pole Street, gave about £700 for it, forthwith shifted thereto, and continue to hold the place.

The building is pretty lofty, and is well galleried. Very lately we were in it, and estimated the number present at 84—rather a small party for a chapel capable of holding 900. It possesses about the best acoustical properties of any place of worship in Preston. The late Mr. Samuel Grimshaw, of Preston, who, amongst many other things, had a special taste for music, used to occupy it at times, with his band, for the purposes of 'practising.' He liked it on account of its excellent sounding qualities. Once, Mr. Grimshaw said he would give the brethren a musical lift with his band during some anniversary services to be held in the chapel. His promise was accepted, and when the day came there was a complete musical flood. The orchestra, including the singers, numbered about 50, and the melodious din they created was something tremendous. There were tenors, baritones, bass men, trebles, alto-singers, in the fullest feather; there were trumpeters, tromboners, bassooners, ophicleideans, cornet-a-piston players, and many others, all instrumentally armed to the very teeth, and the sensation they made fairly shook and unnerved the more pious members of the congregation, who protested against the chapel being turned into a 'concert-hall,' &c. The music after all, was good, and if it were as excellent now there would be a better attendance at the place. The present orchestra consists of perhaps a dozen singers, including a central gentleman who is about the best shouter we ever heard; and they are helped out of any difficulties they may get into by a rather awkwardly-played harmonium.

The Rev. W. J. Stuart is the minister of the chapel, and he receives £70-£80 a year. He has a gentlemanly appearance; looks pretty well considering the nature of his salary. He has fair action, and sometimes gets up to 212 degrees in his preaching. We won't say that he is in any sense a wearying preacher; but this we may state, that if his sermons were shorter they would not be quite so long. And from this he may take the hint.

if his sermons were shorter they would not be quite so long

The admission to either the platform or pulpit of the chapel, not very long ago, of a wandering 'Indian chief,' and a number of Revivalists, who told strange tales and talked wildly, has operated, we believe, against the place—annoyed and offended some, and caused them to leave. The minister, no doubt, admitted these men with an honest intention; but everybody can't stand the war-whooping of itinerant Indians, nor the sincere ferociousness of Revivalists; and awkward feelings were consequently generated in some quarters by them. In the main, Mr. Stuart is a kindly, quiet, gentlemanly person, and barring the little interruption caused by the dubious Indian and the untamed Revivalists, has got on with a small congregation and a bad salary better than many parsons would have been able to do.

Unitarian Chapel

Some of our greatest thinkers and writers have been Unitarians: Milton was one, so was John Locke, and so was Newton. Unitarians generally believe: that the Godhead is single and absolute, not triune; that Christ was not God, but a perfect being inspired with divine wisdom; that there is no efficacy in His vicarious atonement, in the sense popularly recognised; and that original sin and eternal damnation are in accordance with neither the Scriptures nor common sense.

The edifice wherein our Unitarian friends assemble every Sunday, is an old-fashioned, homely-looking, little building. It can be approached by two ways, but it is of no use trying to take advantage of both at once. You would never get to the place if you made such an effort. There is a road to it from Percy Street—this is the better entrance, but not much delight can be found in it; and there is another way to the chapel from Church Street—up a delicious little passage, edged on the right with a house-side, and on the left with a wall made fierce with broken glass, which will be sure to cut the sharpest of the worshippers if they ever attempt to get over it.

The minister, Mr. Orr, is an Irishman, young in years, tall, cold, timid, quiet, yet excellently educated. He is critical, seems slightly cynical, and moves along as if he either knew nobody or didn't want to look at anybody. There is somewhat of the student, and somewhat of the college professor in his appearance. But he is a very sincere man; has neither show nor fussiness in him; and practises his duties with a strict, quiet regularity. He may have moods of mirth and high moments of sparkling glee, but he looks as if he had never only laughed right out about once in his life, and had

repented of it directly afterwards. If he had more dash and less shyness in him, less learned coolness and much more humour in his composition, he would reap a better harvest in both pulpit and general life. He never allows himself to be led away by passion; sticks well to his text; invariably keeps his temper. He wears neither surplice nor black gown in the pulpit, and does quite as well without as with them. For his services he receives about £120 a year and if the times mend he will probably get more.

The singing is only moderate, and if it were not for the good strong female voice, apparently owned by somebody in the gallery, it would be nearly inaudible—would have to be either gently whispered or 'thought out.' The services in the main are simple, free from all boisterous balderdash, and if not of such a character as would suit everybody, are evidently well liked by those participating in them.

simple, free from all boisterous balderdash

The congregation is of a quite genteel and superior character. There are a few rather poor people embraced in it; but nine out of ten of the regular worshippers belong to either independent or prosperous middle class families. They believe in taking things comfortably; never allow their nerves to be shattered with notions about the 'devil,' or the 'burning lake' in which sinners have to be tortured for ever and ever; never hear of such things from the pulpit, wouldn't tolerate them if they did; think that they can get on well enough without them. They may be right or they may be very wrong; but, like all sections of Christians, they believe their own denominational child is the best.

The Free Gospel Chapel

They don't occupy very fashionable quarters; Ashmoor Street, a long way down Adelphi Street, is the thoroughfare wherein their spiritual refuge is situated. If they were in a better locality, the probability is they would be denominationally stronger. In religion, as in everything else, 'respectability' is the charm. We have heard many a laugh at the expense of these 'Free Gospel' folk, but there is more in their creed, although it may have only Ashmoor Street for its blossoming ground, than the multitude of people think of. In the early stages of their existence the Free Gospellers were called Quaker Methodists, because they dressed somewhat like Quakers, and had ways of thinking rather like the followers of George Fox.

About ten years ago, the Preston Free Gospel people got Mr. James Toulmin to build a chapel for them in Ashmoor Street. He did not give them the chapel; never said that he would; couldn't afford to be guilty of an act so curious; but he erected a place of worship for their pleasure, and they have paid him something in the shape of rent for it ever since.

A good view can be obtained from the pulpit. Not only can the preacher eye instantaneously every member of his congregation, but he can get serene glimpses through the windows of eight chimney pots, five house roofs, and portions of two backyards. In a season of doubt and difficulty a scene like this must relieve him.

Their standard is the Bible; they believe in both faith and good works, but place more reliance upon the latter than the former; they recognise a progressive Christianity, 'harmonising,' as we have been told, 'with science and common sense;' they object to the Trinitarian dogma, as commonly accepted by the various churches, maintaining that both the Bible and reason teach the existence of but one God; they have no eucharistic sacrament, believing that as often as they eat and drink they should be imbued with a spirit of Christian remembrance and thankfulness.

Mr. William Toulmin, brother of the owner of the chapel, preaches every Sunday, and has done so, more or less, from its opening. He gets nothing for the job, contributes his share towards the church expenses as well, and is satisfied. Others going to the place might preach if they could, but they can't. He works regularly as a shopkeeper on week days, and earnestly as a preacher on Sundays; passes his life away in a mild struggle with eggs, bacon, butter, and theology; isn't learned, nor classical, nor rhetorical, but possesses common sense; expresses himself so as to be understood—a thing which some regular parsons have a difficulty in doing; and has laboured Sunday after Sunday for years all for nothing—a thing which no regular parson ever did or ever will do. We somewhat respect a man who can preach for years without pocketing a single dime, and contribute regularly towards a church which gives him no salary, and never intends doing. The homilies of the preacher may neither be luminous nor eloquent, neither pythonic in utterance nor refined in diction, but they are at least worth as much as he gets for them. Any man able to sermonise better, or rhapsodise more cheaply, or beat the bush of divinity more energetically, can occupy the pulpit tomorrow. It is open to all England, and possession of it can be obtained without a struggle. Who bids?

Others...might preach if they could, but they can't

The Presbyterians

Some persons fond of spiritual christenings and mystic gossip have supposed that the Presbyterians who, during the past few years, have endeavoured to obtain a local habitation and a name in Preston, were connected with the Unitarians; others have classed them as a species of Independents; and many have come to the conclusion that their creed has much Scotch blood in it. The most ignorant are generally the most critically audacious; and men knowing no more about the peculiarities of creeds than of the capillary action of woolly horses are often the first to run the gauntlet of opinionism concerning them. The fact of the matter is, the Preston Presbyterians are no more and no less, in doctrine, than Calvinists. In discipline and doctrine they are on a par with the members of the Free Church of Scotland; but they are not connected with that church, and don't want to be, unless they can get something worth looking at and taking home.

no more and no less, in doctrine, than Calvinists

In 1866 a few persons in Preston with a predilection for the ancient form of Presbyterianism held a consultation, and decided to start a '*church.*' They had a sprinkling of serious blood in their arteries—a tincture of well-balanced, modernised Puritanism in their veins—and they honestly thought that if any balm had to come out of Gilead, it would first have to pass through Presbyterianism, and that if any physician had to appear he would have to be a Calvinistic preacher.

In September, 1867, the Rev. A. Bell, a gentleman young in years, and fresh from the green isle, who pleased the Preston Presbyterians considerably, was requested to stop with them and endeavour to make them comfortable. Mr. Bell thought out the question briefly, got a knowledge of the duties required, &c., and then consented to stay with the brethren. And he is still with them; hoping that they may multiply and replenish the earth, and spread Presbyterianism muchly.

There is no pulpit in the building [the theatre of Avenham Institution], and the preacher gets on very well is the absence of one. If he has no pulpit he has at least this consolation that he can never fall over such a contrivance, as the South Staffordshire Methodist once did, when in a fit of fury, and nearly killed some of the singers below. The congregation consists principally of middle and working class people. Their demeanour is calm, their music moderate, and in neither mind nor body do they appear to be much agitated, like some people, during their moments of devotion.

The preacher, who has been about six years in the ministry, and gets £250 a year for his duties here, is a dark-complexioned sharp-featured man—slender, serious-looking, energetic, earnest, with a sanguine-bilious temperament. He is a ready and rather eloquent preacher; is fervid, emphatic, determined; has moderate action; never damages his coat near the armpits by holding his arms too high; has a touch of the '*ould Ireland*' brogue in his talk; never loudly blows his own trumpet, but sometimes rings his own bell a little; means what he says; is pretty liberal towards other creeds, but is certain that his own views are by far the best. Like the rest of preachers he has his admirers as well as those who do not think him altogether immaculate; but taking him in toto—mind, body, and clothes—he is a fervent, candid, medium-sized, respectable-looking man, worth listening to as a speaker of the serious school, and calculated, if regularly heard, to distinctly inoculate you with Presbyterianism.

43

Christian Brethren

In all large towns a few of this complexion may be found; and in Preston odd ones exist whose shibboleth is 'Christian Brethren.' We had a spell with them, rather unexpectedly, on a recent 'first day' —Christian Brethren always call Sunday the first day. And it came about in this way: we were on the point of entering a Dissenting place of worship, when a kindly-natured somewhat originally-constituted 'pillar of the Church' intercepted our movements, and said, "You mustn't come here today." "Why?" we asked, and his reply was, that a fiftieth-rate stray parson, whom "the Church doesn't care for" would be in the pulpit that day, and that if we wished for "a fair sample" we must "come next Sunday." We didn't want to be hard, and therefore said that if another place could be found for us, we would take it instead. Violent cogitation for five minutes ensued, and at last our friend, more zealous than erudite, conjured up what he termed, "them there new lot, called Christians."

At our request he accompanied us to a small, curiously-constructed building in Meadow Street. At the side of the doorway we observed a strangely-written, badly-spelled sign, referring to the different periods when the 'Christian Brethren' met for worship, &c. Hurrying up fourteen steps we reached a dark, time-worn door, and after pausing for a moment —listening to some singing within —our guide, philosopher, &c., opened it, and we entered the place with him. The room was not 'crowded to suffocation;' there were just fourteen persons in the place—four men, three women, two youths, a girl, and four children. A Bible and a hymn book—the latter, according to its preface, being intended for none but the righteous—were handed to us, and our friend went through the singing in a delightfully-dreadful style. He

appeared to have a way of his own in the business of psalmody—sang whatever came into his head first, got into all manner of keys, and considering that he was doing quite enough for both of us, we remained silent, listening to the general melody, and drinking in its raptures as placidly as possible.

Like the Quakers, Christian Brethren are a 'peculiar people.' They believe more in being good and doing good than in professing goodness formally. They recognise some forms and a few ceremonies; but vital inherent excellence—simple Christianity, plain, unadorned, and earnest—is their pole-star. They claim to be guided in all their religious acts solely by the Scriptures; consider that as 'the disciples were first called Christians at Antioch,' their followers have no right to assume any other name; think, baptismally speaking, that whilst there may be some virtue in sprinkling and pouring, there can be no mistake about absolute immersion, inasmuch as that will include everything; think baby baptism unnecessary, and hold that none except penitent believers, with brains fairly solidified, should be admitted to the ordinance; maintain that, as under the apostolic regime, 'the disciples came together on the first day of the week to break bread,' Christians should partake of the sacrament every Sunday; call their ministers 'evangelists;' hold that at general meetings for worship there should be full liberty of speech; that worship should be perfectly free; and that everything should be supported on the voluntary principle.

44

The Tabernacle of the Revivalists

"It's a regular bird nest, and you'll never get to it, unless you ask the neighbouring folk," said a friend to us whilst talking about the Revivalists' tabernacle. To the bottom of Pitt Street we then went, and seeing two or three females and a man dart out of a dim-looking passage beneath one of the side arches of the railway bridge there, we concluded that we were near the *'nest.'* We never saw such a time-worn and dumfounding road to any place, and if those who patronise it regularly had done their best to discover the essence of dinginess and intractability, they could not have hit upon a better spot than this. A warm air wave, similar to that you expect on entering a bakehouse, met us just when we had passed the wooden partition. In the centre of the room there was a stove, almost red-hot. This apartment, which was filled with small forms, was, we ascertained, a Sunday School. At the bottom end there were some narrow steps, leading through a large hole into a room above —the *'chapel.'* A fat man could never get up these steps, and a tall one would injure his head if he did not stoop very considerably in ascending them.

The chapel is about five yards wide, 15 yards long, very low on one side, and moderately high on the other. It is plain, rickety, and whitewashed. The side wall of the railway bridge forms one end of it. On the northern side, there is a door fastened up with a piece of wood in the form of a large loadstone. This door leads to the top of a pig-stye. The *'chapel'* will hold about 70. When we visited it, the congregation consisted of 35 children of a very uneasy sort, 11 men, and five women. Every now and then railway goods trains kept passing, and what with the whistling of the engines, the shaking caused by the waggons, the barking of a dog in a yard behind, the grunting of a pig in a stye three yards off, and the noise of the 35 children before us, we had a very refreshing time of it.

The congregation—a poor one—consists of a remnant of the Revivalists who were in Preston last year, and it has a kind of nominal connection with the Orchard United Methodists They are an earnest body, seem obliging to strangers, are not as fiery and wild as some of their class, and might do better in the town if they had a better room. They have no fixed minister. The preacher we heard was a stranger. He pulled off his coat just before beginning his discourse. After a few introductory remarks, in the course of which he said he had been troubled with stomach ache for six hours on the previous day, and that just before his last visit to Preston he had an attack of illness in the very same place, a lengthy allusion was made to his past history. He said that he had been *"a villain, a gambler, a drunkard, and a Sabbath breaker"*—we expected hearing him say, as many of his class do, that he had often abused his mother, thrashed his wife, and punished his children, but he did not utter a word on the subject. The remainder of his discourse was less personal and more orthodox. At the close we descended the steps carefully, groped our way out quietly, and left, wondering how ever we had got to such a place at all, and how those worshipping in it could afford to Sabbatically pen themselves up in such a mysterious, ramshackle shanty.

Cannon Street Independent Chapel

Cannon Street Chapel has neither a bell, nor a steeple, nor an outside clock, and it has never yet said that it was any worse off for their absence. But it may do, for chapels like churches are getting proud things now-a-days, and they believe in both lacker and gilt. There is something substantial and respectable about the building. It is neither gaudy nor paltry; neither too good nor too bad looking. Nobody will ever die in a state of architectural ecstasy through gazing upon it; and not one out of a battalion of cynics will say that it is too ornamental. It is one of those well-finished, middle-class looking establishments, about which you can't say much any way; and if you could, nobody would be either madder or wiser for the exposition.

no common Dissenting rendezvous for ill-clad screamers and roaring enthusiasts

The interior of Cannon Street Chapel has a spacious and somewhat genteel appearance. A practical business air pervades it. There is no *'storied window,'* scarcely any *'dim religious light,'* and not a morsel of extra colouring in the whole establishment. At this place, the worshippers have an idea that they are going to get to heaven in a plain way, and if they succeed, all the better—we were going to say that they would be so much the more into pocket by it. Freedom of thought, sincerity of heart, and going as straight to the point as possible, is what they aim at. There are many seats in Cannon Street Chapel, and, as it is said that hardly any of them are to let, the reverend gentleman who makes a stipulated descent upon the pew rents ought to be happy. It is but seldom the pews are well filled: they are not even crammed on collection Sundays; but they are paid for, and if a congenial wrinkle does not lurk in that fact—for the minister—he will find neither the balm of Gilead nor a doctor anywhere. The clerical notion is that pew rents, as well as texts must be stuck to; and if those who pay and listen quietly acquiesce, then it becomes a simple question of *'so mote it be'* for outsiders.

The congregation is made up of tolerably respectable materials. It is no common Dissenting rendezvous for ill-clad screamers and roaring enthusiasts. Neither fanatics nor ejaculaters find an abiding place in it. Not many poor people join the charmed circle. A middle-class, shopkeeping halo largely environs the assemblage. There is a good deal of pride, vanity, scent, and silk-rustling astir in it every Sunday, just as there is in every sacred throng; and the oriental, theory of caste is not altogether ignored. But the bulk are of a substantial, medium-going description—practical, sharp, respectable, and naturally inclined towards a free, well got up, reasonable theology. There is nothing inflamed in them, nothing indicative of either a very thick or very thin skin. Any of them will lend you a hymn book, and whilst none of them may be inclined to pay your regular pew rent, the bulk will have no objection to find you an occasional seat, and take care of you if there would be any swooning in your programme.

The genteel portion of the congregation principally locate themselves in the side seats running from one end of the chapel to the other; the every day mortals find a resting place in the centre and the galleries; the poorer portion are pushed frontwards below, where they have an excellent opportunity of inspecting the pulpit, of singing like nightingales, of listening to every articulation of the preacher, and of falling into a state of coma if they are that way disposed.

Cannon Street Independents — Music & Ministry

The music at this place of worship has been considerably improved during recent times; but it is nothing very amazing yet. There is a certain amount of cadence, along with a fair share of power, in the orchestral outbursts; the pieces the choir have off go well; those they are new at rather hang fire; but we shall not parry with either the conductor or the members on this point. They all manifest a fairly-defined devotional feeling in their melody; turn their visual faculties in harmony with the words; expand and contract their pulmonary processes with precision and if they mean what they sing, they deserve better salaries than they usually get. They are aided by an organ which is played well, and, we hope, paid for.

The minister is the Rev. H. J. Martyn, who has had a good stay with '*the brethren*,' considering that their fighting weight is pretty heavy, and that some of them were made to '*have their way*.' Frequently Independents are in hot water concerning their pastors. In Preston they are very exemplary in this respect. The Grimshaw Street folk have had a storm in a tea pot with one of their ministers; so have the Lancaster Road Christians; and so have the Cannon Street believers; and the beauty of it is, they generally win. Born to have their own way in sacred matters, they can turn off a parson, if they can't defeat him in argument. And that is a great thing. They hold the purse strings; and no parson can live unless he has a '*call*' to some other '*vineyard*,' if they are closed against him. On the whole, the present minister has got on pretty evenly with his flock. He has had odd skirmishes in his spiritual fold; and will have if he stays in it for ever; but the sheep have a very fair respect for the shepherd, and can '*paint the lily*' gracefully. A while since they gave him leave of absence—paying his salary, of course, whilst away—and on his return some of them got up a tea party on his behalf and made him a presentation. There might be party spirit or there might be absolute generosity in such a move; but the parson was no loser—he enjoyed the out, and accepted with Christian fortitude the gift.

The Rev. H. J. Martyn is a small gentleman–considerably below the average of parsons in physical proportion; but he consoles himself with the thought that he is all right in quality, if not in quantity. Diminutive men have generally very fair notions of themselves; small men as a rule are smarter than those of the bulky and adipose school; and, harmonising with this regulation, Mr. Martyn is both sharp and kindly disposed towards himself. He is not of opinion, like one of his predecessors, that he assisted at the creation of the world, and that the endurance of Christianity depends upon his clerical pivot; but he believes that he has a '*mission*,' and that on the whole he is quite as good as the majority of Congregational divines.

> It is only when the thermometer is rising that you enjoy him

The level places in his sermons are rather heavy, and, at times, uninteresting. It is only when the thermometer is rising that you enjoy him, and only when he reaches the climax and explodes, that you fall back and ask for water and a fan. He gets well paid for what be does—last year his salary exceeded £340; and our advice to him is—keep on good terms with the bulk of '*the brethren*,' hammer as much piety into them as possible, tickle the deacons into a genial humour, and look regularly after the pew-rents.

The Mormons

Preston features prominently in the history of the Mormons — The Church of Jesus Christ of Latter-day Saints. Because of the remarkable early growth of membership here in the 1830s, the area was chosen for the site for England's second temple, which was erected in Chorley and dedicated in June 1998. Hewitson wrote extensively about the origins of the Mormons, and their arrival in Preston. He expressed these contemptuous opinions of their beliefs:-

On the 22nd of September, 1827, a rough-spun American, named Joseph Smith, belonging to a family reputed to be fond of laziness, drink, and untruthfulness, and suspected of being somewhat disposed to sheep-stealing, had a visit from *'the angel of the Lord.'* He had previously been told that his sins were forgiven; that he was a *'chosen instrument,'* &c., and on the day named Joseph found, somewhere in Ontario, a number of gold plates, eight inches long and seven wide, nearly as thick as tin, fastened together by three rings, and bearing inscriptions, in *'Reformed Egyptian,'* relative to the history of America *'from its first settlement by a colony that came from the Tower of Babel at the confusion of tongues, to the beginning of the 5th century of the Christian era.'* These inscriptions, originally got up by a prophet named Mormon were, as before stated, found by Joseph Smith, were read off by him to a man rejoicing in the name of Oliver Cowdery, and they constitute the contents of what is now known as the *'Book of Mormon'*. The language is quaint and simple in syllabic construction; but the book altogether is a mass of dreamy, puzzling history—is either a sacred fiction plagiarised, or a useless and senile jumble of Christian and Red Indian tradition.

There are about 1,100 different religious creeds in the world, and amongst them all there is not one more energetic, more mysterious, or more wit-shaken than Mormonism. It is a mass of earnest *'abysmal nonsense,'* an olla-podrida of theological whimsicalities, a saintly jumble of pious stuff made up—if we may borrow an idea—of Hebraism, Persian Dualism, Brahminism, Buddhistic apotheosis, heterodox and orthodox Christianity, Mohammedanism, Drusism, Freemasonry, Methodism, Swedenborgianism, Mesmerism, and Spirit-rapping. We might go on in our elucidation; but what we have said will probably be sufficient for present purposes.

...an olla-podrida of theological whimsicalities, a saintly jumble...

Smith, the founder of Mormonism, had only a rough time of it. His Church was first organised in 1830, in the State of New York. Afterwards the Mormons went into Ohio, then established themselves in Missouri, were next driven into Clay County, subsequently look refuge in Illinois, and finally planted themselves in the valley of the great Salt Lake, where they may now be found. Smith came to grief in 1844, by a pistol shot, administered to him in Illinois by a number of roughs; and Brigham Young, a man said to be *'very much married,'* and who will now be the father of perhaps 150 children, was appointed his successor.

The Mormons in Preston

In 1837, certain elders of the Mormon Church, including Orson Hyde and Heber C. Kimball, were sent over to England as missionaries; the first town they commenced operations in, after their arrival, was—PRESTON; and the first shot they fired in Preston was from the pulpit of a building in Vauxhall Road, now occupied by the Particular Baptists. Things got hot in a few minutes here; it became speedily known that Hyde, Kimball, and Co. were of a sect fond of a multiplicity of wives; and the '*missionaries*' had to forthwith look out for fresh quarters. They secured the old Cock Pit, drove a great business in it, and at length actually got about 500 '*members.*'

Whilst this movement was going on in the town, the missionaries were pushing Mormonism in some of the surrounding country places. At Longton, nearly everybody went into raptures over the '*new doctrine;*' Mormonism fairly took the place by storm; it caught up and entranced old and young, married and single, pious and godless; it even spread like a sacred rinderpest amongst the Wesleyans, who at that time were very strong in Longton—captivating leaders, members, and some of the scholars in fine style; and the chapel of this body was so emptied by the Mormon crusade, that it was found expedient to reduce it internally and set apart some of it for school purposes. To this day the village has not entirely recovered the shock which Mormonism gave it 30 years ago. During the heat of the conflict many Longtonians went to the region of Mormondom in America, and several of them soon wished they were back again. In Preston, too, whilst the Cock Pit fever was raging, numbers '*went out.*' After the work of '*conversion,*' &c., had been carried on for a period in the sacred Pit mentioned, the Mormons migrated to a building, which had been used as a joiner's shop, in Park Road; subsequently they took for their tabernacle an old sizing house in Friargate; then they went to a building in Lawson Street now used as the Weavers' Institute, and originally occupied by the Ranters; and at a later date they made another move—transferred themselves to a room in the Temperance Hotel, Lime Street, which they continue to occupy, and in which, every Sunday morning and evening, they ideally drink of Mormondom's salt-water, and clap their hands gleefully over Joe Smith's impending millenium.

Extracts from a Newsquest Media Group report in February 1998:

Up to 200, 000 visitors are expected at Chorley's new multi-million pound Mormon temple when it throws its doors open to the public this spring. The complex — built on a 15-acre site at Hartwood Green, by junction 8 of the M61 — is the largest project of its kind carried out by the Church of Jesus Christ of Latter-Day Saints in the entire world.

The church came to this country in 1837 and the Preston branch is the oldest continuous branch of the church anywhere.

The Preston Temple is already a local landmark. It has a white granite building featuring a gold-leafed statue of an angel on top of its lone spire. The site incorporates a number of other buildings, including a chapel for use by both local and regional congregations, a training centre, accommodation and offices. The temple has around 150 rooms and includes a massive baptismal font sitting on the back of 12 life-size oxen, representative of the 12 tribes of Israel.

Attending a Mormon service in the Temperance Hotel

There were just six living beings in the room—three well-dressed moustached young men, a thinly-fierce-looking woman, a very red-headed youth, and a quiet little girl. Then in stepped a strong-built dark-complexioned man, who marched forward with the dignity of an elder, until he got to a small table surmounted by a desk, whence he drew a brown paper parcel, which he handed to one of the moustached young men, who undid it cautiously and carefully, "*What is it going to be?*" said we, mentally; when, lo! there appeared a white table cloth, which was duly spread. The strong-built man then dived deeply into one of his coat pockets, and fetched out of it a small paper parcel, flung it upon a form close by, seized a soup plate into which he crumbled a slice of bread, then got a double-handled pewter pot, into which he poured some water, and afterwards sat down as generalissimo of the business. The individual who manipulated with the table cloth afterwards made a prayer, universal in several of its sentiments; but stiffened up tightly with Mormon notions towards the close.

Two elderly men and a lad entered the room when the orison was finished, and a discussion followed between the '*general*' and the young man who had been praying as to some hymn they should sing. "*Can't find the first hymn,*" said the young man; and we thought that a pretty smart thing for a beginning. "*Oh, never mind, go farther on—any long metre,*" uttered his interlocutor, and he forthwith made a sanguine dash into the centre of the book, and gave out a hymn. The company got into a '*peculiar metre*' tune at once, and the singing was about the most comically wretched we ever heard. The lad who came in with the elderly men tried every range of voice in every verse, and thought that he had a right to do just as he liked with the music; the elderly men near him hummed out something in a weak and time-worn key; the woman got into a high strain and flourished considerably at the line ends; the little girl said nothing; the three young men seemed quite unable to get above a monotonous groan.

Speaking succeeded; they all eulogised in a joyous strain the glories of Mormonism, but never a syllable was expressed about wives. A young moustached man led the way. He told the meeting that he had long been of a religious turn of mind; that he was a Wesleyan until 17 years of age; that afterwards he found peace in the Smithsonian church; that the only true creed was that of Mormonism; that it didn't matter what people said in condemnation of such creed; and that he should always stick to it. The thin woman, who seemed to have an awful tongue in her head, was the second speaker. She panegyrised '*the church*' in a phrensied, fierce-tempered, piping strain, talked rapidly about the '*new dispensation,*' declared that she had accepted it voluntarily, hadn't been deceived by any one—we hope she never will be—and that she was happy. Her conclusion was sudden, and she appeared to break off just before reaching an agony-point.

the singing was about the most comically wretched we ever heard

Quakers' Meeting House

A building located somewhere between Everton Gardens and Spring Gardens was first used as a meeting-house by them. In 1784 a better place was erected by the Friends, on a piece of land contiguous to and on the north side of Friargate; and in 1847 it was rebuilt. Although no one was officially engaged to map out the place, a good deal of learned architectural gas was disengaged in its design and construction. It was made three times larger than its congregational requirements—the object being to accommodate those who might assemble at the periodical district meetings. Special attention was also paid to the loftiness of the building—to the height of its ceiling. One or two of the amateur designers having a finger in the architectural pie had serious notions as to the importance of air space. They had studied the influence of oxygen and hydrogen, of nitrogen and carbonic acid gas; they had read in scientific books that every human being requires so many feet of breathing room; and after deciding upon the number of worshippers which the meeting-house should accommodate, they agreed to elevate its ceiling in the ratio of their inspiring and expiring necessities. This was a very good, salutary, Quakerly idea, and although it may have operated against the internal appearance of the building it has guaranteed purity of air to those attending it.

The meeting house is a quiet, secluded, well-made place; but it has a poor entrance, which you would fancy led to nowhere. A stranger passing along Friargate on an ordinary day, would never find the Quakers' meeting house. He might notice at a certain point on the north-eastern side of that undulating and bustling public thoroughfare a grey looking gable, having a three-light-window towards the head, with a large door below, and at its base two washing pots and a long butter mug, belonging to an industrious earthenware dealer next door; but he would never fancy that the disciples of George Fox had a front entrance there to their meeting house. Yet after passing through a dim broad passage here, and mounting half a dozen substantial steps, you see a square, neat-looking, five-windowed building, and this is the Quakers' meeting house.

Over the passage there is a pretty large room, which is used by the Friends for Sunday school purposes. The attendance at this school on ordinary occasions is about 60. During the Cotton Famine, a few years ago, when the Quakers were manifesting their proverbial charity—giving money, food, and clothing—the attendance averaged 160; and if it was known that they were going to give something extra tomorrow it would reach that point again. Speaking of the charity of Quakers, it may not be amiss to state that they keep all their own poor—do not allow any one belonging their society ever to solicit aid from the parish, or migrate in the dark hour of poverty to the workhouse.

The inside of the general building is severely plain. There is no decoration of any description about it, and if the gas pipes running along the side walls had not a slight Hogarthian line of beauty touch in their form, everything would look absolutely horizontal and perpendicular. The seats are plain and strong with open backs. There is no pulpit in the house, and no description of books—neither Bibles, nor hymn-books, nor prayer-books—can be seen anywhere.

Quakers in Worship

At the head of the place there is an elevated strongly-fronted bench, running from one side to the other, and below it an open form of similar length. The more matured Quakers and Quakeresses generally gravitate hitherwards. The males have separate places and so have the females. It is expected that the former will always direct their steps to the seats on the right-hand side; that the latter will occupy those on the left; and, generally, you find them on opposite sides in strict accordance with this idea. There is nothing to absolutely prevent an enraptured swain from sitting at the elbow of his love, and basking in the sunlight of her eyes, nor to stop an elderly man from nestling peacefully under the wing of his spouse; but it is understood that they will not do this, and will at least submit to a deed of separation during hours of worship.

You can feel the quietude, see the stillness

They have two meetings every Sunday, morning and evening, and one every Thursday—at half-past ten in the morning during winter months, and at seven in the evening in summer. The average attendance at each of the Sunday meetings is about 70. The character of the services is quite unsettled. Throughout Christendom the rule in religious edifices is to have a preliminary service, and then a discourse; in Quaker meeting houses there is no such defined course of action. Sometimes there is a prayer, then another, then an 'exhortation'—Quakers have no sermons; at other times an exhortation without any prayer; now and then a prayer without any exhortation; and occasionally they have neither the one nor the other—they fall into a state of profound silence, keep astonishingly quiet ever so long, with their eyes shut, and then walk out. This is called silent meditation. If a pin drops whilst this is going on you can hear it and tell in which part of the house it is lying. You can feel the quietude, see the stillness; it is sadly serene, placidly mysterious, like the 'uncommunicating muteness of fishes;' and you wonder how it is kept up. To those who believe in solemn reticence—in motionless communion with the 'inner light,'— there is nothing curious in this; it is, in fact, often a source of high spiritual ecstacy; but to an uninitiated spectator the business looks seriously funny, and its continuance for any length of time causes the mind of such a one to run in all kinds of dreadfully ludicrous grooves.

Quakers don't believe in singing, and have no faith in sacred music of any kind. They have no regular ministers, and allow either men or women to speak. None, except Quakers and Ranters—the two most extreme sections of the religious community, so far as quietude and noise are concerned—permit this; and it is a good thing for the world that the system is not extended beyond their circles. If women were allowed to speak at some places of worship they would all be talking at once—all be growing eloquent, voluble, and strong minded in two minutes—and an articulative mystification, much more chaotic than that which once took place at Babel, would ensue.

At the meeting house in Friargate it is taken for granted that on Sundays the morning service lasts for an hour and a half, and the evening one an hour and a quarter; but practically the time is regulated by the feelings of the worshippers—they come and go as they are 'moved,' and that is a liberal sort of measure harmonising well with human nature and its varied requirements.

At the conclusion of his final piece in the *Chronicle* on 11th December 1869, Hewitson wrote

"We have finshed. Before long we shall commence another series of sketches. But for the present it is all over—the lime lights are burning, the coloured fires are radiating their hues, the curtain is falling, and, bidding "Adieu" to all our kind readers, we vanish."

But, perhaps to the disappointment of some of the clergy who had been *'appraised'* (some may even have thought they had been *'lampooned'*) in the last few months, he didn't vanish at all. Only a few days had elapsed before, on 24th December 1869, Hewitson offered for sale a book containing all the articles, almost exactly in the form in which they had appeared in the *Chronicle*. His introduction said that they were written in "*a lively spirit, which may be objectionable to the phlegmatic, the sad-faced, and the puritanical*". He continued "*Those who don't care for the gay will find in these sketches the grave; those who prefer vivacity to seriousness will meet with what they want; those who appreciate all will discover each. The solemn are supplied with facts; the facetious with humour; the analytical with criticism.*"

The carefully selected extracts on the preceding pages provide many examples of these special qualities, but there is much more to be found in the book itself. In particular, there is a wealth of information on the general history of each place of worship in Preston, claimed by the author to be "*fuller and more reliable than any yet published.*" We strongly recommend the whole book for further reading, and though it may be difficult to locate a copy to purchase, there are many available through libraries, particularly in and around Preston.

OUR

Churches and Chapels,

THEIR

Parsons, Priests, & Congregations ;

BEING A

CRITICAL AND HISTORICAL ACCOUNT

OF EVERY PLACE OF WORSHIP

IN PRESTON.

BY " ATTICUS "

(A. HEWITSON)

———

'T is pleasant through the loopholes of retreat
To peep at such a world.—*Cowper.*

———

Reprinted from the Preston Chronicle.

———

PRESTON :
PRINTED AT THE " CHRONICLE " OFFICE, FISHERGATE.
1869.

Anthony Hewitson by C Sanderson of Preston
*Property of Martin Duesbury, great-grandson of AH
and used with his permission*

**The front cover of the new collection of articles
covering churches and chapels
in the countryside around Preston.
The engraving is of Stydd, described as
*"the oldest Lancashire church, founded in the 12th century"***

Announcement of a New Project

Following the success of his survey of churches in Preston, Hewitson announced, in the *Chronicle* of May 7th 1870, his intention to visit many of the country churches and chapels around Preston. He began: '*Into the country we have now got, and we can breathe freely. We leave behind all that is vicious, and tiresome, and inodorous, — the bustling streets with their noise and glare, town competition with its fierce whirl and strategy, the reeking court where gin is god and fighting law, the back alley, with its lairs of sin and poverty, the capacious square on whose parapets beggars creep and cringe, and in whose gardens the emerald of nature is dulled by the smoke of a thousand chimneys — all these do we retire from, and come at once, with a quiet salaam, into the country during this 'merry month of May', flowers, and birds, and foliage are hastening merrily into new life, giving a beauty to the scene which the genius of art cannot touch, and which man can only wonder at and admire.*' After these colourful words he ventured first only as far as Penwortham, just a stone's throw from Preston! Thereafter, his sketches appeared weekly in the *Chronicle* until February 3rd 1872. Soon after, on March 2nd 1872, this advertisement appeared offering his collected sketches under the title '*Our Country Churhes and Chapels*'.

The book amounted to nearly 600 pages containing around 300,000 words. This is the brief preface:

The sketches in this volume originally appeared in the Preston Chronicle. Many of them — the bulk — were written amid the turmoil of 'business,' and under circumstances precluding that calm and isolation so essential to literary operations. They are republished in book form, for the convenience of the public and the benefit of the Author, who thinks it is far better to speak candidly than to adopt the fashionable plan of apologising for a literary enterprise, or fabricating reasons for appearing in print. When first printed, these sketches were eagerly read by many persons; and the belief is entertained that, in their revised and reconstructed form, they will meet with a favourable reception. They embrace subjects for all sections of readers; contain historical, antiquarian, and critical matter to be found in no other volume; and the author, who has to thank many gentlemen for the ready and courteous manner in which they have supplied him with information, now leaves the work to stand by its merits or fall by its defects.

NOW READY.
In Book form, 580 pages, with a
BEAUTIFULLY PHOTO-LITHOGRAPHED
FRONTISPIECE,
Our
"COUNTRY CHURCHES AND CHAPELS,"
Being a reprint, carefully revised and enlarged, of the well known rural sketches,
BY "ATTICUS."
The work embraces the History, Traditions, Curiosities, and most striking features, past and present, of the following places, along with an authentic account of their Churches, Chapels, Schools, Parsons, Priests, &c.:

Ashton.	Fernyhalgh.	Poulton-le-Fylde.
Alston.	Freckleton.	Pilling.
Bamber Bridge.	Grimsargh.	Rawcliffe.
Bretherton.	Goosnargh.	Rufford.
Brindle.	Garstang.	Ribchester.
Brownedge.	Great Eccleston.	Singleton.
Barton.	Heapey.	Scorton.
Broughton.	Hesketh Bank.	Samlesbury.
Bonds.	Hambleton.	Stalmine.
Bowgrave.	Inskip.	St. Michael's.
Bleasdale.	Inglewhite.	Tarleton.
Croston.	Kirkham.	Treales, Roseacre, &
Clayton Green.	Knowl Green.	Wharles.
Churchtown.	Longridge.	Warton.
Claughton.	Longton.	Wray Green.
Caldervale.	Leyland.	Westby.
Chipping.	Lea.	Weeton.
Catforth.	Lund.	Whitechapel.
Cottam.	Lee House (Thornley)	Whittle.
Eccleston.	Much Hoole.	Wheelton.
Euxton.	Mawdesley.	Walton (Higher and
Elswick.	Nateby.	Lower.)
Fulwood.	Newsham (Newhouse)	Woodplumpton.)
Farington.	Penwortham.	&c., &c.

A Book for the cheerful and the grave, the serious and the humorous; full of choice descriptions and unique criticisms; and an
EXCELLENT WORK OF REFERENCE,
more complete than any yet published, for all residing in the districts above mentioned.

PRICE, IN NEAT CLOTH, 5s.; IN CRIMSON AND GOLD, 7s. 6d.

Orders must be given *early*, at the "Chronicle" Office, Preston, or through the Booksellers, as *only a limited number of copies has been printed.*
The History of the Churches and Chapels of Preston, by "Atticus," (Price 2s.; half calf 3s.), forms a companion volume to the above, and may also be obtained at the "Chronicle" Office, Preston.

TRAVELLING INTO THE COUNTRYSIDE

There were some time-consuming train journeys from Preston.

To Calder Vale & Bleasdale

Exactly as the Sunday morning train for the north began to move out of Preston Station we rushed into that peculiar edifice, hurried towards a carriage, entered it, permitted our breath to reach a fair level, and then looked round. A bright winter sun was shining outside; a cheerful company was chatting inside; and the conversation was at least varied, if not edifying—it referred to potatoes, municipal elections, and religion; and as we were nearing Garstang station it took a quick turn in the direction of railway mechanism, and ended in somebody saying that the past week had been an eventful and unparalleled one in the history of the Garstang and Knot End Railway, inasmuch as there had not been a break down on that said little and most ill-starred junction during the previous six days. It is considered that there is something seriously wrong on this junction if the engine or something pertaining to the direct working of the line does not get out of order once a week, or oftener; hence the astonishment manifested at the proper conduct of things on it for the long and trying period of about 60 hours.

A slow journey to Bamber Bridge in winter

Snow fell, sleet fell, rain tried to fall, but couldn't: nobody seemed to be fairly and legitimately awake; and those who were up appeared to have shook themselves out of sleep by mistake. The ticket man at the station was cold—blew his fingers with his breath before he gave us a card; the guard looked shivery, and apparently required '*nourishment;*' the porters seemed grim and starved; the station-master had a frosted-up appearance; the engine-driver had a chill upon him. There was a wintery desolation about the carriages; everything seemed to be below freezing point. The first carriage offered by the porter was dingy, smelled of rum, tobacco, and other aromatic agents. After finding another suitable place, we sat .... expecting—for the carriage never moved an inch—to be at the end of our pilgrimage some time during the year. A shout, two or three railway fingers held up, a sharp whistle, and a quick jerk followed; and in ten minutes we got to a flat sort of place which a passer-by, on the platform, dressed in new corduroy, called '*Bomer Brig.*' This was Bamber Bridge.

A train to Lea

.....seemed to know it was Sunday, and had conscientious scruples about running—didn't know whether to hang on at Preston and think out the question, or start and do its best. It moved 55 minutes after its advertised time, the bulk of the passengers having been waiting in it three-quarters of an hour; it proceeded 40 yards; then it stopped, and moved back about a yard; then it went forward another yard; then it got a fresh idea into its head, and turned back again; and just as somebody was saying "*This here train is the blessedest concern I were ever in,*" it started in earnest, and landed us, in about five minutes, at Lea. Two milk cans, a couple of women, a red-headed man, and the writer of this article got out at Lea, and all of them seemed to breathe more freely when emancipated from that wearisome caging-up in carriages.

Delays, and some very dull company

"*Rufford?*" said we, nodding at a railway carriage forming one of a train of twelve, standing alongside the eastern platform of the Preston station. "Yes," answered a radiant-faced guard, and the quick style in which he got rid of that small word, made us believe that the train was on the very edge of moving. But it wasn't. We sat still for five minutes wasting the moments of a valuable life; then read a polemical book for five minutes; then for five minutes surveyed the cimmerian roof of the old station; afterwards for five minutes tried to find relief in the board advertisements fixed opposite the carriage, and involving the quintessence of incongruity—cock and hen feeding compounds, wine cellar frames, turnip manure recommendations, college prospectuses, furniture vans, brandy bottles, stoves, anti-bilious pills, &c; then had ushered into our presence a solitary and exactly-moulded swell; for five minutes we looked obliquely at him, but found no comfort in the creature; then got into an introspective mood, as philosophers would call it, for five minutes; and at the expiration of that time the train was off. Evenly and rapidly did it move along; but we had small comfort, for we had little company, in the journey. There was, to be sure, the solitary swell; but he, like all swells, was too fine and too incipient for our taste. Not a word did he utter. For a moment or two he concentrated his mind upon his boot laces—got them tight and regular and then, during the remainder of the passage, he entered into a painfully-precise rectification of his finger nails—cut them round evenly, rubbed them delicately, scraped them tenderly, polished them thoroughly, and just when we were on the point of imagining that he would be pulling out a microscope to examine them, a stout voice shouted out "*Rufford.*"

We emerged from the carriage instantly, leaving the lone swell to solve in his own peculiar fashion the great and momentous finger nail question. What a clean, sweet, rural-looking station this is, said we, mentally, after the train had moved onwards and we had got a chance of surveying the place. And how select and quiet it is! was the thought which followed. At some country stations, on a Sunday in particular, you are annoyed and '*faced out*' by gossipping, lounging, inanely-staring gangs of young men and lads, who saunter up from the village, eye you from hat to shoes, laugh like idiots if you are dressed contrary to their own traditional ideas of propriety, and discuss the colour and cut of your top-coat for long enough after you have gone out of sight. Croston station is one of the worst in the country for this sort of thing. Extremes, however, meet; so at the very next station—Rufford—we experience a quietude and a serenity, a stillness and a freedom, most distinct in appearance, and most refreshing in its influence.

A '*wonderful obliging*' station master

On leaving Warton we retraced our steps to Wray Green; the nearest railway station, for our purpose, being there. We reached the old village, which is about 200 yards from the station, a few minutes before train time; and were hurrying through it very rapidly when one of the natives, whose house we were passing, shouted out, "*Ah, you needn't hurry; they're wonderful obliging at th' station; if th' driver or th' owd station master saw you or anybody else going up th' road they'd stop th' engine.*" But we got to the place in time, although if late we might have experienced the accommodating qualities of the railway people; for we have seen the driver pull up here, after starting, to let a person get into a carriage.

No connection to Garstang on Sunday

Out of the dull Sunday morning town, with only horn-thumbed milkmen, and mufflered dog-fanciers, and suspicious *'thirsty souls'* astir; over a complicated number of railway points, with sharp, saucy, engine-whistles assailing one's ears every other moment; then a quickening movement by dismal-looking cottages, grim saw-pits, and lofty-sided mills; and then we have a clear-breathing space in the country, with green fields and cattle on each side, and hills filling up bravely and beautifully the eastern horizon; gentlemen's residences breaking in upon the view occasionally; sundry glimpses of a roundabout, obsolete canal; tempting views of hares and rabbits, with a stately-walking pheasant now and then thrown into the bargain; periodical sights of fish-ponds, with broad yellow flowers, and quick-witted little water-hens floating amongst them; a swift penetration into a shadowy wood, whose branches and foliage seem to be opening out with a wild rustle for the flying train; a return of daylight and free breathing space; a whistle; and in a few moments afterwards a stoppage. This is about the sum and substance of a journey by train from Preston to what is called Garstang Station—an elevated, exposed place, on the main line, about two miles from the town of Garstang, and recently connected with that said town by a poor little junction, which runs to Pilling, and winds up in a field there. We expected being able to catch a train on this small contribution to railway science for Garstang; but the station-master informed us we could not—said that not a single train ran upon it on a Sunday; so we had to walk. At first we set down this closing up of the little junction to some special spell of piety or Puritanism, to a desire on the part of the directors to get to heaven quicker than all the other railway folk, except those saints who live in Scotland; but we subsequently learned that the directors were not so very punctilious after all—that, in fact, their line was kept quiet on the Sunday, not because it was sinful to run trains on that day, but because if the trains were run they would **not pay**!

To Wray Green by train

Wray Green is on the south-eastern side of Westby, and you get to it, after leaving Kirkham, by one of the queerest little cork-screwy, junction railways in the kingdom. Directly after diverging from the main road, you swerve suddenly on one side, and then feel as if you were either going over the hedge, or back to Kirkham again. You get to a right-angled position with the chief road in a twinkling, dart into a steep little cutting, wind about like a salmon scaling a fish ladder, and wonder wherever the driver is going to, and whether in the end he will come to a dead stand, or run carefully into the side, or land you in a field. But we found the driver, who was in charge of a tiny old-fashioned locomotive, decorated with as much shining brass as a Saturday afternoon chimney piece, and with as many taps and knick-knacks all over as half-a-dozen of those concerns out of which bar-maids pump ale, to be a wide awake fellow; he had all the ups and downs, and turns, and gradients of the road off by heart—went as placidly through the labyrinth as if he had served a ten years' apprenticeship to blind-fold wheelbarrow racing, and in a minute or so he landed us at the Lilliputian, rustic-looking station of Wray Green, where a fatherly old man, of homely, weather-beaten aspect took our ticket, and allowed us to *'pass.'*

Recognised on the way to Lund Church West of Preston, about five miles, there stands a little, cleanly-got-up place called '*Salwick station*'. '*Fine fooak*,' as Tim Bobbin would say, sound the '*l*' in that name; ordinary souls, who have to get through the world in a rough-and-ready fashion, leave it out, and pronounce the word as '*Sowick*,' or '*Sahwick*.' At this diminutive wayside station we arrived, by a long Sunday morning train, containing many who were going onward to enjoy the sea air, and marine scenery, and salutary pleasures of Lytham and Blackpool, saying nothing of the bottled beer and whisky recreations of those favourite watering places. We stood still upon the platform till the train departed, and then met with a broad-set, weatherbeaten man, in his shirt sleeves—like an old coasting '*salt*'—who took our ticket, told us the way to Lund Church, and then, with a merry twinkle in his eye, said, "*Are you gooing to give them a lifter?*"

At Eccleston (*the pub landlord was asked if he would..*) "*See when the trains go from Euxton and Croston to Preston.*" The radiant landlord, with his best Sunday shirt on, courteously disappeared to consult all the time tables, and in about a quarter of an hour he returned, and said, "*Ah don't see't. I've lookt in t' Ormerick [almanack] and can't find it.*" We found no fault; for a man who patiently looks in the '*Ormerick*' for train arrivals and departures is worthy of our best and broadest sympathy.

Finding the way to Pilling Any one unacquainted with the district, who can get to Pilling comfortably, is a genius, and fit to head an Arctic expedition. We landed there after much inquiring, cross-questioning, and tribulation; and when we got there we had to wander all round the spot before we could find it.

Travelling by road could be expensive A drive to Freckleton is pleasant—we found it so—and yet there is a multiplicity of odds and ends in the work detracting somewhat from the comfort of it. We ride along very gallantly during the first half of the journey; and just when we are beginning to admire the scenery right and left—run into raptures respecting woody landscapes, and swell into a '*fine phrenzy*' regarding rich flocks and winding waters,—we are suddenly confronted by a strong blue-eyed damsel at a toll gate, who shouts out "*Three-pence!*" The money was paid at once, and away we went down hill, to the left, and along a circuitous lane, flanked with sundry fields, containing divers partridges, till at length we got abreast of another gate. There seemed to be nobody about it, and this gate, we imagined, would be one of the cheap kind. But, by a sort of magic, there suddenly sprang out of a little hut at the road side a small boy, who ran to the gate, opened it, and then looked up with an expectant eye for '*something*.' A coin was thrown to him, and he pulled his cap peak thankfully. Having passed this gate, we were upon what is called '*Freckleton Marsh*'—a broad, tolerably green tract of land—upon which were many calves and heifers fond of rambling upon the road, and very stupidly inclined when shouted at to get out of the way. In less than ten minutes yet another gate was reached, and out came a woman, with a demand for fourpence. The gate was only a small one, and when we handed out the money, and intimated that the gate ought to be far larger—that we were getting very little for the money—she smiled, and began to defend the dimensions of the aforesaid gate.

There was a boy at yet another gate, but it turned out that this was not a compulsory affair, although very sanguine expectations of what Eastern spongers term '*bakshish*' were entertained.

Croston

St Michael's Church The congregation seemed to extract more pleasure out of two or three christenings which were gone through in the middle of the service than anything else. The screaming of the youngsters made them look, and laugh, and wink at one another wonderfully, and when this was over their curiosity was excited by the marching up to the chancel of two or three women, who had made up their minds to undergo a *'churching'* process. The congregation we saw was numerous, respectable in attire, and in the main very orderly. There were a few lively hobbledehoys—as there are in all country churches—behind where we sat, who for a time plagued a buxom young girl considerably. She sang with a sweet vigour when the music started, and when she got very rapturous the lads said, "*Well done, Mary.*" She smiled, but went on, and when they said "*Go it, Maria,*" she got still more earnest, and in the end subdued by her perseverance her rollicking criticisers, and actually got all of them singing with her.

United Methodist Church A young man was playing agonisingly upon a little and most wind-shaken harmonium fixed within a railed enclosure in front of the pulpit. On one side of him were three stout young females without bonnets, wearing long white brats, and short-sleeved frocks, out of which their strong, plump, red arms emerged at the sides very patently. One of them had a short red shawl over her shoulders; another had a brown one similarly fixed; the third was content with her long white brat for a covering. On the other side of the harmonium player there was a quiet female in black, and near her an official kind of young fellow, who chimed in at the singing. Over the choir rails half a dozen youngsters were climbing and making noises. In a corner to the left of the pulpit there was a melancholy old man, who was afterwards joined by a pleasanter-looking, grandfatherly sort of person, and three children. Upon a form in front of the pew there was lying at full length a little lad, wearing a corduroy suit, with five-and-twenty brass buttons upon his jacket. Half-a-dozen children sat on forms before the choir rails; and a dismal-looking woman sat on the far side, about eight inches off a large stove, making a dismal effort to warm herself. Her propinquity to the stove, which would have melted down into a jelly a fat person, did not seem to affect her in the least, and after an hour's roasting she had still a shivering look.

She sang with a sweet vigour .....and actually got all of them singing with her

Wesleyan Chapel ...the matter of the sermon is practical, the manner of its delivery is vehement and rather violent at times. The preacher, who has a heavy tragedy voice, gives the fullest play to his lungs, keeps everybody wide awake, and flings his hands about very briskly. Sometimes he quavers them sharply, then lifts the Bible nearly over the front of the pulpit, then replaces it, and comes down upon it in a strong sledge-hammer style, almost sufficient to drive in the front of the desk. And in this way he keeps on for five and thirty minutes, alternately delighting and stunning the congregation; and finally sits down, nearly out of breath, with a face red and shiny with sweat, and with a consciousness that he has done his duty. On the whole, and barring the uproar of its delivery, the sermon was one of the best we had for some time heard in a little country chapel.

Chipping

The village is five miles north-east of Longridge, occupies a very sequestered position, stands high up, at the base of Parlick Pike, and embraces in its population as vigorous a class of workers and ale drinkers as you will find within the northeastern boundary of Lancashire. There is a saving faith in Lord Derby hereabouts; his lordship owns much property in the district; under his house particular families have for generations tenanted the same lands and occupied the same dwellings; they are never disturbed if they at all behave themselves; nor is their rent ever raised—it is *'the same yesterday, to-day, and for ever,'*—and whilst this system naturally obtains for Lord Derby the character of a *'capital landlord,'* it is a question with many persons whether it does not check enterprise, cramp energy, and deprive the locality of that productiveness which under a sharper regime it would be certain to manifest.

Catholic Chapel The Rev. John de Gryse came to the mission in 1865. Mr. de Gryse is a tall, slender, youthful looking gentleman; he can twist his features in all ways, and can perhaps talk better with his face, without opening his mouth, than any gentleman you ever met with. His difficulty with the English language—he is a Belgian—has, no doubt, developed his facial gesticulation. He is about 35 years of age, and was born at Ghent, in Belgium, educated and ordained there, and afterwards came to St. Joseph's, Manchester, where he remained for three years, and then proceeded to Chipping. He is shrewd, careful of a very inquiring

Father de Gryse

turn of mind, quiet, and believes in labouring earnestly, and minding his own business. The only fault we had to find with the church during our visit was, that it was singularly cold. There was a keen December frost outside, and when we entered the chapel we espied a powerful looking stove, and got close to it; but our hopes were blighted—the article had nothing in it. During the service we several times got close to the borders of starvation, and if the zeal of the general congregation had not been very warm, the shivering would have been quite enormous.

St Bartholomew's Church The congregation we saw was numerous, quiet, and yet fond of looking about: it was formed of fatherly old farmers, some of whom wore knee breeches and blue stockings, ancient matrons with ancestral shawls and bonnets on, buxom young lasses, and blithe, strong young fellows, who could break in a floor with hornpipe dancing, or sit down and sup ale till all was blue; there were also polished-looking young people of both sexes present, and amongst the gathering were many uneasy children, who could not be kept quiet on any account; coaxing did them no good; ear-pulling did not pacify them; so they had their way to the end. The church-wardens sat in a closed pew at the higher end of the south aisle, and with their wands of office near them looked as potent as Grand Brahmins, and as official as if they had each been superintendent of the County Constabulary. The singing was only moderate; the instrumental music—harmonium playing—was not entrancing. But then one has no right to expect marvels in melody at such an *ultima thule* part of the world.

St Mary's Church, Eccleston

On entering the church we find it expansive, clean, capital in its arrangements, but rather gloomy. By and by a bulky gentleman, with an air of authority about him, walks into the church. This is the rector; then farmers and young men and comely females follow, taking up their seats in various quarters; afterwards a harum scarum set of lads—scholars apparently—rush into the building, and find seats in the north western corner; a thin, learned-looking, wiry gentleman—the curate—next puts in an appearance, walking up the centre aisle, with a serious sort of swing, to the vestry; a weighty good-looking lady, with a lot of courage in her, and a brisk flash in her eye—she looked like the rectoress—then went to the boys and gave them a quiet lecture; and in a few minutes the service commenced. The scholars were a particularly intractable class, and they defied all the efforts of a young man sitting close by, to keep them quiet. He had a singularly energetic and uneasy time of it: first he shook his head at them; but that would not do; then he *'shooshed'* them, making sounds like those caused when you jirk up the safety-valve of a boiler, but that was ineffectual; afterwards he got hold of a long stick and rattled the heads of the youngsters with it, and then they assumed a moderate attitude of quietness; but an uneasy soul remained in them to the last, and if you had knocked the whole lot down and fastened them to the floor, they would in some way have manifested their restlessness.

It was said that the ringers were *'on strike,'* and there was evidently *'something up,'* for only four of the six bells were rung. A notice in the church porch stated that, at a vestry meeting, it had been resolved that each ringer on absenting himself from duty, morning or evening, unless sick or unable to find a substitute, would have to submit to a deduction of 3d. from his salary. The ringers, some of whom had been in the habit of *'slipping out'* during service time, would not stand this, and hence a sort of strike ensued. A minute fixed below the notice named, clearly showed that there had been trouble in past times through this *'slipping out'* business. It was dated September 17, 1815, and stated that a representation had been made to the minister and churchwardens that some of the ringers, after pulling the bells prior to service in the church, went away; that this was very indecent and prejudicial to religion; and that in future the ringers must attend divine service morning and evening.

The rector is the Rev. John Sparling—a cheerful, portly, well-educated gentleman, full of good humour, and as far removed from straight-lacedness as bliss is from perdition. He is beautifully fat, tolerably fair, and five years on the shady side of 50. His exact weight is 192 lbs. avoirdupois; his height will be about 5 ft. 4 in.; and his breadth about 3ft. 1in. He has a globular, shrewd, shiny, Israelitish look—is easy, plucky when roused, can preach a good sermon; sleeps well; makes a quiet country magistrate; has a clear net income of about £1,100 a year, and receives it with due Christian resignation. The sermon was preached by the curate, and the moment he began about half of the members of the congregation turned their heads round and looked at a dim little clock perched over an arch just above where we were sitting. That was a plain hint to the preacher that he must pay due deference to the question of time during his discourse.

He got hold of a long stick and rattled the heads of the youngsters with it

St. Mary's Church, Goosnargh

The congregation is pleasant-looking and well attired, but very slender, numerically speaking. About 100 visit the church in the morning, and between 30 and 40 in the evening. We saw this number at each service; but then it was, perhaps, not a right day to take—there were collections on hand, and they have always a centrifugal influence. Owing to certain differences, the attendance generally has been reduced considerably of late, and a little Wesleyan Chapel with a new front to it, about a quarter of a mile from the village, has received into its bosom several of the dissatisfied ones.

Goosnargh Wesleyan Chapel

This place, if we accept ordinary rumour, has played the deuce with the church—has taken away many of its worshippers, blossomed northwards, owing to insufficient accommodation, about three yards, and crossed the Jordan of general success. The building is small, is fronted with iron rails and two scrapers, and, more remotely, with nine loads of broken stones, and is flanked with what seems to be a snug, new shippon. There are no particular historic associations about this place. It has a capacity for about 120 persons; is nearly empty every Sunday morning, and full every Sunday afternoon; has no regular minister; owns about ten even-going Sunday scholars; possesses some robustious singers on the male side; is a neat, clean building; contains numerous ancient prayer-books, four smart lamps, a good pulpit, and two really first-class hat-rails.

Freckleton Wesleyan Chapel

The preacher was a thoroughgoing Mr. Blazeaway—a savagely-earnest, desperately shouting, strangely Bible-hitting, tremendously-sweating soul. If the entire universe had been only a quarter of an inch off general and irretrievable ruination, and if the grand Ruler of the universe had been deaf and millions of miles away, the preacher could not have shouted more vehemently, nor dashed into the pulpit top with his fists more vigorously. We can put up with a tolerable amount of shouting—something equal to about 100 lbs. on the square inch; but when it gets to about 300 lbs. we feel nervous, and consider that escape is necessary.

For this and other reasons we retired before the service was over—went to a gate, had a little quiet enjoyment in inspecting some cows—and then returned to make an examination of the chapel. We entered the first pew, and found that the only occupants of the building were three men, in an out-of-the-way corner, engaged in praying. They were earnest souls, and we kept a respectful silence. At the finish one of them shouted out *"Have you come to take part in the meeting?"* We gave a negative reply, referred to the character of our mission, and were treated with courtesy.

> The preacher was savagely-earnest, desperately shouting, strangely Bible-hitting

Longton

"They're a queer lot, the Longtoners," said a coolly-humorous man to us, and when we asked how that was he continued, *"They're the queerest lot alive; nearly every one of them wears clogs, and you may tell them in a minute when they leave home, for they stare about at everything like nick'd uns, and gape like young throstles."* This was rather a rough, unclassical description, and it would probably have been truer 20 years ago than now, for during our visit nine out of every ten persons we met were respectably dressed, and, on the whole, kindly and courteous in their manners. In old times Longton, which in appearance was no better than a snipe bog, with deep ditches on each side of its main road, was a supremely rough place —an awful place for fighting and drinking, and quite impervious to the regular influences of civilisation. If a missionary had been sent into the place in those times he would not, perhaps, have been eaten, but he would have been stoned out in a twinkling, and if any body had found fault with the process, they would have been similarly treated. The people, however, are now living under a better and more wholesome regime; and yet we know there are still some curious beings in Longton—specially rough, don't-care-for-anybody sort of folk—rudely-vigorous, harum-scarum souls, who don't want to know anything about parsons, and who would glory in hammering policemen right out of existence. The village of Longton is now one of the prettiest in the country. There are numerous small cottages in it; they seem all clean and tidy; many have attached to them little gardens; and the bulk have flowers growing about them. The better class houses in the village have a cozily-genteel appearance—are partially shrouded with trees, and have roses and honeysuckles creeping up their walls.

Wesleyan Chapel The average attendance on a Sunday is equal to the capacity of the chapel, and if it were larger there would be more at it; for one of the chief officials informed us that there was not a sitting to let, and that there were upon the books applications for *'whole pews.'* The congregation we saw was numerous, was made up largely of working people, and was very respectable in appearance, and very orderly in demeanour—had no religious *'fits,'* screamed none, groaned not at all—indeed, was quieter and more seemly in its conduct, during the most exhilarating periods, than many Dissenting congregations in large towns where it is considered good taste and a higher range of civilisation prevail.

Primitive Methodist Chapel The singing gave us the horrors; it was started by a fierce shouting man, who commenced the tune, sustained it to the end of the second line, then forgot all about it, and handed over the job to the preacher. Two young men, sitting beneath the cupboards, with their feet stretched out towards an old cracked stove, had a very happy time of it; they laughed and winked much, and a couple of young women in the back-ground, who apparently understood all about it, did the same thing.

St Andrew's Church There was a numerous congregation when we were at the church; and both modern and ancient times were duly represented in the dresses of those present. In hats there was much diversity: one old blade, sitting towards the north-western corner, had the biggest castor we ever had the pleasure of seeing. The pew he sat in would just hold the hat and its owner; and how he got the article through the doorway without asking for help, puzzles us. In old times —yes, within the past 80 years— females guilty of improper conduct had to go to the church in white garments, and do penance for their irregularities!

Penwortham

Hereabouts Nature seems complete; wild flowers bloom in profusion; the air is redolent of Flora; the speckled thrush sings out its lays amid the adjoining bushes; the linnet twitters and hops from branch to branch; the swift-winged swallow skims along the avenue sides merrily; the stately blackbird parades the grass busily and silently; now and then a hare or rabbit darts through the underwood; the brown partridge and the richly-hued pheasant may occasionally be seen in the immediate neighbourhood; whilst all around scenery of the sweetest and loveliest description presents itself. A long and most beautiful avenue, umbrageous and shadowy, constitutes its approach. On the lower side of the Preston and Liverpool road, and not far from the entrance to the avenue, there is a spring of water, which runs into an oblong stone trough, and which for generations has gone by the name of 'St. Mary's well'. Many people, particularly Irish, assign to its water miraculous properties. The well is now closed over, and has only a pipe in front. This alteration was made a few years ago, in consequence of the manner in which Irish and other people polluted the water by washing themselves in it.

St Mary's Church Those attending the church constitute a peculiarly mixed congregation: you have the village boy in corduroy, and the rural hobbledehoy in awkward-fitting three-and-sixpenny-a-yard cloth; the ploughman with his speckled, bright-coloured neckerchief, and the rustic maiden, who has begun fixing up her hair in town style; the antique, rough-shod farmer, with long hair reaching straight down in a level line to his eye-brows, and the cleanly-clad rural matron, with modest bonnet, and long broad cap-strings; the County Court judge, sitting calmly, like Gamaliel, on one side, with the halo of authority about him; squires,

rubicund, homely, and aristocratic are there, too; so is Jeames the footman, with his drab suit, scarlet facings, and finely brushed-up head of hair; so also is the irrepressible youngster, who must be carried out by the elder sister once or twice during the service. We look round, and see representatives of each of the classes mentioned; then we look ahead, to the chancel and notice just two human beings — the incumbent, sad and potential in the corner, and the squire of the parish with a bright flower in his coat collar, sitting at his ease not far from the reading desk. The place wherein we see him located is ancient, runs back into the centuries, bears many traces of quaint by-gone days. The members of the choir are very good singers for a country church. It would be an improvement if they were permitted to intone the responses, which at present are 'talked' —done in a very dull, rumbling distant-thunder sort of way.

The salary of the incumbent is only small: he gets about £150 a year. Mr. Rawstorne is about 45 years of age and edits that morning star of bucolic literature 'The Penwortham, Longton, Farington, and Balderston Parish Magazine;' Mr. Rawstorne has a curate whose name is Herbert Martyn Endo Tattershall. That is rather a lengthy name for one human being to put up with; but then this is a world of trial, and we must all be patient, 'for in due season we shall reap if we faint not.' It may be interesting to the good people of Penwortham to know that however long may be the name of their curate in the English language, it is a flea-bite in comparison with what it is in some tongues: in Malagasy, for instance, it runs in this fine style —'Ramapirapiratratranoratsiana'. His parishioners ought to be thankful that the Malagasy nomenclature has not yet been introduced amongst them.

Irish and other people polluted the water by washing themselves in it

Two admired 'mill' villages

Scorton is situated in Nether-Wyersdale, stands at the base of a picturesque range of hills, and has a most quiet and contented appearance. The village ought to be the happiest in all England, for it has neither a public-house, nor a beer-shop, nor a doctor, nor a lawyer, nor a policeman in it! Some places cannot thrive at all without these adjuncts of *'civilisation;'* physic, drink, law suits, and handcuffs seem to be essential to their welfare; but Scorton, very correctly termed *'the model village,'* feels perfectly content without having such things in its midst. And yet it can't do without some of them; it requires pills and potions occasionally, and sends to Garstang, or Lancaster, or Preston for them; it feels inclined for a drop of something now and then, and slips over to the *'Old Holly,'* or the *'New Holly,'* or the *'Middle Holly'* —all public houses on the *'border land;'* and it has sometimes to consult a lawyer. There used to be a beerhouse in the village, on the northern side, near the mill; and some years ago a building was erected on the other side for public-house purposes; but the beershop was given up and the other building named never got opened as a public-house. Both places are now converted into cottages. Scorton is a somewhat talented, curious, and go-ahead place; it has got a good brass band; it has gas, a public clock, a Maypole, a church and a chapel, a cotton factory, a whale's jawbone put up like an arch, and many other useful and odd things.

Calder Vale is one of the prettiest villages we have seen. It is deeply set, romantically situated; the air from the mountains wafts gently over it; the shadowy beauty of a wooded glen environs it; and through its midst there runs with murmuring music the stream of the Calder.

> it has neither a public-house nor a beer-shop, nor a doctor, nor a lawyer, nor a policeman in it

You may travel many miles and not meet with such a pleasing place as this; it is sequestered, scenic, cheerful, a kind of oasis amid the hills, and beautiful in its isolation. This village was founded in 1835 by Messrs. Richard and Jonathan Jackson, who built a cotton mill along the edge of the Calder, and of course had to erect houses for the accommodation of those working in it. The population have neither a public house, nor a beerhouse, have neither a lawyer nor a doctor amongst them, and although they do happen to have a policeman, he is mainly required for other places, and would die of starvation and a broken heart if he had to depend for a living upon the business he does at the village of Calder Vale. The entire place is owned by the Jacksons, and they won't have anything in the shape of a beershop or public-house in it.

On a Sunday you do not on that day see the young women—like the virgins of some manufacturing villages—hanging about door-steps with shawls over their heads, and wearing long coarse brats reaching from their chins to their clog toes; nor the young men pitching and tossing, and hugging dogs through back alleys, and carrying baskets with pigeons in them through fields; nor the old women gadding about in dirty caps, retailing as much scandal in five minutes as would put a fairly-sized town into confusion for a month if it got fairly into circulation; nor the old men sitting all day through in their working clothes, nursing their heads after a Saturday night's spree; nor the children darting in and out, and all over, without shoes or stockings; no, the population here is clean and orderly, and an air of self respect appears to run through the whole place.

The Willows Catholic Chapel, Kirkham

The *'district'* of the Willows has a great Catholic population. Altogether, there are about 1,900 in it. There are at present at least eight times more Catholics in the district than there were at the beginning of this century. The increase has mainly taken place during the past 20 years—an increase, no doubt, largely caused by the great influx of Irish people into the district within the time specified.

Father Hines is a robust, well-developed, cheerful-featured gentleman; has healthy, smiling, agricultural-looking cheeks; a clear smooth forehead, thin spare hair, a penetrating yet humorous eye; likes snuff, books, and little children; is clear headed and active; has a lively stock of anecdotes, ranging from metaphysics to tame ferrets; makes himself comfortable all round; looks after his mission very industriously; and enjoys the respect and esteem of all about him. The Rev. Roger Taylor, his assistant, is a broadish-set, compactly made gentleman. He has strongly-defined, steadily-balanced features; has a cool, immobile, contemplative eye; reminds you, when you catch his profile, of somebody wonderfully like either Bishop Goss or Napoleon I; if he looked over a hedge at you with a mitre on you would swear he was the former; if he peeped in at the door with a general's hat on you would certainly have an idea that the latter had reappeared.

The Willows
From an engraving in the Preston Chronicle, 26 April 1845

Heapey Church

Here the congregation was very small, around 100 in a church with a capacity for 950. This was because ....a misunderstanding arose between the late Rev. J. Fisher, who was incumbent of the church at the time, and some of the congregation who had serious grievances to complain of; many of the people, including some of the most influential, left the place........ *The 'split' had occurred only four years before his visit, but in that short time a new church had already been built at nearby Wheelton for a congregation of 400. It was known as:*

Wheelton Free Church of England

The service we were present at was thoroughly Protestant, strictly Church of England, without either the heavy dullness of the *'low'* party, or the aesthetic eccentricity of the *'high'* section. The singing was melodious, vigorous, and went off in some parts like a hurricane. We never heard any class of singers throw themselves—body, soul, shoes, and stockings—more earnestly into the business of vocalisation than those at Wheelton Church. They have got voice-power enough to drown ten big drums, fifteen little ones, and many clarionettes, and if they had only a little more sweetness, they would be completely captivating. The organ playing was as perfect as one had a right to expect it at such a place as Wheelton; and the organ blowing was done by a curious old fellow, who used to raise the wind at Heapey Church, and who thinks he has a special gift for blowing. He looks daft; but if you had to offer him sixpence and a penny, and tell him he might take one of them, he would fall foul upon the sixpence.

A Primitive Methodist camp meeting at Wharles

As we were leaving Treales, a friend, who happened to be in the district, overtook us, and on his mentioning that there was going to be *"a grand stir amongst the Ranters,"* at Wharles, in the afternoon, we decided to retrace our steps. We may here observe that there are numerous Primitive Methodists in Wharles and the neighbourhood; that this denomination has long had a footing hereabouts; that the nearest chapel for them is at Catforth; and that the Primitives of Wharles, on certain nights during the week, have cottage meetings in their own hamlet. The *'camp meeting'* we have mentioned was held on a green hemmed in with gardens and thatched houses; and from all quarters we saw men, women, and children, dressed in their *'bitter best'* flocking to it. A red cart constituted the platform of the speakers.

When we reached the place there would be a congregation of about 160, which increased considerably afterwards. Many *'hearers'* were standing in front of the cart; some were leaning against it; one was sitting underneath it; a few women and old people were reposing contentedly in chairs; odd ones were ducking down under the hedge; others were looking up from behind it; and in the distance there were batches of young fellows with their hands in their pockets, chewing tobacco quietly, winking at the young women who passed, and smiling half-critically at an old gentleman—a superannuated preacher with a mackintosh on—who was holding forth in the cart. He talked about the antiquity of Primitive Methodism, said it was as old as Moses, and wound up by an appeal to the shiners present to be virtuous. A young man, sitting at the back of the cart, then had a spell of talking; and then an older man, who complained of having a weak chest, but made the welkin ring again, said something. Subsequently the speakers walked in processional order to the centre of the green, formed a circle, and began singing and praying. The proceedings here were more lively than they were in the cart; some of the brethren got enthusiastic and excitable; shouted more keenly; and threw themselves into more rapturous attitudes. One old man burst into a fine phrensy several times, and shouted *'Glory'* often. In about ten minutes there was a return to the cart, and then the old man shouted out, *"Come here, lasses,"* but he was checked by the brother with the mackintosh on, who said it didn't matter where they stood on the ground, and next began condemning some young people in the background most violently, for manifesting indifference towards the proceedings. After more talking, and a little more singing, the affair was brought to a close by an intimation that in the evening there would be a *'Love Feast'* in brother some-body's barn.

At the Love Feast: After the men had let out the nature of their sinfulness and bliss, by the experience-telling process, an effort was made to induce the women to do likewise. *"Will some sister say a word now?"* said a meek voiced man in one corner of the barn. Never a *'sister'* spoke—not one of them even said how old she was; they looked with a quiet cunning, as much as to say that weasels were not going to be caught asleep on that particular occasion, and we rather admired their sagacity. What business was it of Brother Snoozlemoutofit or any other brother to know the wickedness or joyfulness of a bevy of good-looking young females and matured matronly women?

St. Michael-le-Wyre Church

The service had just begun, but we got not a pinch of comfort out of it, owing to the excessive coldness of the place. On turning round, perhaps in half an hour after entering the building, we suspected that the door through which we had passed was open, for we could see trees and a wall at the outside through an aperture between its two folds. Partly through his own chilliness, and partly through a hint we made, a friend sitting next to us got up, said, "*I'll shut it*," and walked to the door. In a moment afterwards he returned, and said "*It's shut—but I could nearly shove my foot through it.*" Turning to the left we noticed another door, and it was just as awkwardly made as that named, for over the top of it we could see trees, &c., in the churchyard. What is meant by such like doors we cannot tell; all we really do know is, that the cold which generally prevailed drove three upright men, after the service, to the sinful business of drinking gin and hot water at the '*Brown Cow*', and prompted one of the number to swear that the Archdeacon ought to stand glasses round for the martyrdom they had gone through! This was highly irreverent talk; but there is much of that kind of language used in these degenerate days, and we simply mention the above as a fact, and not by way of approving of it.

St Michael's Church
(from *Northward* by A Hewitson)

Archdeacon Hornby was born at St. Michael's Vicarage, in 1810; studied at Christ Church, Oxford; afterwards returned home; became vicar in 1847 was made a canon in 1850; and archdeacon in 1870. He is a pretty tall, moderately slender, very gentlemanly-looking person; walks with a brisk lively tread, and can walk much easier without his archdiaconal gaiters and apron than with them; doesn't care an inch for said gaiters and apron, and would as soon wear a proper hat as the one he got when he donned that kind of armour; has a clear, fresh-as-the-morning face, with sparkling, round, sharp-stirring eyes; has a clear-keyed voice; likes good horses, and good carriages, and tenants who pay their rent well; uses an eye-glass much—keeps lifting it up and down—when reading in the church, and handles that same article elegantly when preaching, but this is entirely a work of supererogation, as he always preaches without even notes; stands steady and stately in the pulpit; is mild, and orthodox in his general discourses; is a man whom you can '*sit under*' very comfortably, for he will never horrify you, and never drive you into a state of phrenitis; goes along coolly, carefully, easily; might with advantage throw a little more force into his homilies; is an extraordinary penman, once nearly killed two newspaper reporters whilst attempting to decipher the manuscript of a churchwarden's charge of his, and has often sent into despair, with parcel directions, the station master of Brock; believes in smooth sailing, and quiet skies, and roseate sunsets, although we once did see him at Blackpool,— he having gone thither one wild morning to look at a storm; is well-bred, scholarly, placidly-aristocratic, candid, cute, and cheerful. His church living is worth about £700 a year, and he has a good income from private property.

Ashton Church

Gentlemen of good position, farmers, tradesmen, labouring people, and others of similar social status form the congregation. The sermon was rather dry and quiet in tone, and on carefully considering the matter, we think that about three persons were listening to it; the rest were doing gentle sleeps on their own account, viewing the walls quietly, or wandering about, mentally, in a very dazed and vacuous fashion. We noticed three lawyers sitting in the body of the church asleep.

Wray Green Church

"What a swellish congregation!" whispered a companion of ours, and there was no mistake about it—at any rate so far as the gentler sex were concerned. Many of the children, too, were wonderfully smart. Of course there were in this congregation, as there are in all country assemblies, plain homely-looking men and women—men with rough, honest hands, heavy shoes, and old fashioned handkerchiefs round their necks, women with grandmotherly bonnets and gingham umbrellas, broad-faced lads, who like falling asleep as soon as ever the sermon begins, and stalwart young fellows, hearty as bucks, with necks tanned dark red by the sun, and with heads like haystacks surmounting them. Still, whilst balancing up these beings, you cannot remove the impression that the congregation is, on the whole, a smart one, has a spicy *tout ensemble f*or the district, and in fact has more real bib and tucker about it than can be seen in nineteen twentieths of ordinary country churches. The service was regularly gone through; and the periodical bowing was in certain cases quite superb. At some places we have seen, when the name calling for reverence was mentioned, men nodding their heads as if they were just recognising somebody on the opposite side of the street, and females ducking down quickly all in a lump like charity school girls; but here we noticed the '*correct thing*'—the elegant descent, the long drawn, evenly-pulled bend, the easy drawing-room debut undulation, taking a quarter of a minute to get through it; and the ordinary folk were rather inclined to be select and slowly-fine in their motions.

Catforth Primitive Methodist Chapel

The congregation is formed for the most part of agricultural people—farmers, their wives, farm servants, &c., all fairly dressed, and very sociable in disposition. The service was gone through with less boisterousness, and more calm earnestness, than we anticipated. Occasionally there was a little sighing and a fraction of serious groaning; once or twice odd members of the congregation got into a fine phrensy and shouted out vehemently as if somebody had fastened them to the floor and were bruising them badly; but in the main, the service was decorously and sincerely participated in; it had very little of that roaring roughness, that fiery storminess about it which may be observed in some out-of-the-way country chapels when the steam is fairly turned on. The old lions and the young ones do roar here at times; but we were glad to notice that the congregation generally did not turn the place into anything like a menagerie, and that, in the aggregate, they were calm and placidly reverential. Just after the sermon was commenced a halt took place in order that a number of lads, sitting in front of the pulpit, who were falling asleep in a general heap, might be stirred up and rearranged. They were all leaning against one another, with their eyes closed, and if the end one on the inner side had given way, they would all have fallen over like a row of bricks.

Odds and Ends

Samlesbury Church The font is between 700 and 800 years old. It stands on one side of and just within the principal doorway at the south west corner of the church; is plain, circular, massive, made of a closely-grained sand-stone, and contained, when we lifted the lid—an old trowel, a paint can, two ancient rags, four sticks, a piece of blue paper, a lump of stone, and sundry other articles equally interesting and valuable. The christening pew near it contained some good old shovels, several rollers, sticks, paint cans, &c. The churching pew adjoining had no '*ornamentation*' of this description in it; but in time, if all is well, it may have.

Euxton Church We had a quiet peep into the pulpit, and then thought of the past— thought of the discovery once made in it. There was found some years ago, in this identical pulpit, under the floor, not a skeleton, nor the philosopher's stone, nor a bagful of old coins, nor a swarm of fugitive bees, nor the mouth of a subterranean passage, but—what? —listen!— '*be still, wild heart!*' —why, there was actually found in it a whisky still! And a very spiritual thing, too. Yes, somebody had secreted, we were going to say, a real live, but if not that, certainly a first-rate whisky-spinning apparatus in the poor, old, innocent pulpit.

Claughton Catholic Church Father Barrow was a former priest here whom the Vicar of Chipping once offended in some way, and Barrow vowed that if he ever caught him he would horse-whip him. Well, the Vicar happened to turn up one fine day in some part of the district, and, having ascertained this, Barrow set off to administer the promised castigation. In the meantime, the Vicar had got an inkling of the approaching Nemesis, and he lost no time in shifting his quarters.

Father Barrow gave chase some distance, but fright put mettle into the movements of the Vicar, who escaped rapidly to his own native hills.

Westby Voluntary labour was called upon by Father Hines to build a new Catholic church in 1859. The farmers lent their horses and carts, and many, too, of the Protestant neighbours, kindled by the excitement of the occasion, and their own kind and neighbourly generosity, gave Mr. Hines, on many occasions, the use of their carts and horses.

Bonds, Garstang When Father Michael Hickey died in 1871, his funeral was attended by people belonging all denominations; and old, quaint-minded Garstang, which, for want of better diversion, had burnt him in effigy on many a Fifth of November night, closed the shutters of its shops and wept whilst his ashes were being put into the grave.

Singleton Church In 1578, according to a record in the Chester Presentments at York, the curate of Singleton just did as he liked—seemed to care for nobody, and managed things any way. "*Ther is not servyse done in due tyme. He kepeth no hours, nor releveth the poore. He is not dyligent in visitinge the sycke. He doth not teach the Catechisme. There is no sermons. He churcheth fornycatours without doinge any penaunce. He maketh a dongehill in the chapell yeard, and he hath lately kepte a typlinge hous and a nowty woman in it.*" This was a beautiful state of affairs—eh? The neglect of preaching, and visiting, and teaching, and the making of a midden in the chapel yard were awkward enough; but that '*typlinge hous*' and that '*nowty woman in it,*' were awfully refreshing novelties to be under the superintendence of a curate.

What came next?

Between the summers of 1872 and 1875, Hewitson wrote for the *Chronicle* a series of articles entitled *"Sights and Incidents or Places and Faces"* which were published in book form in 1875. They covered a huge variety of topics and places. One, entitled *"A Talk and a Smoke with a Philosopher"* describes a visit to London to meet Thomas Carlyle, the famous Scottish satirical writer and essayist. A somewhat prejudiced view of Preston appeared at the outset of the conversation:

"You come from Preston?" he said, and on our replying in the affirmative he rejoined—*"Priest-town—are there many Roman Catholics in it?"* We replied that there were between 30,000 and 40,000 in the town, and this seemed to impress him with the idea that Preston was not a very promising town. Identifying Preston with a murky, densely-smoky atmosphere, he next began speaking upon the evil of what we recognise in large towns as the *'smoke nuisance,'* and said that all who polluted the atmosphere with smoke were enemies of the people's health, and ought, in every case, to be prosecuted.

"Carlyle....showed no hesitation in talking, seemed to keep back nothing, chatted in a surprisingly friendly and spirited fashion, and left upon our mind, by personal contact, an impression we had previously formed by perusing his writings—that he was a singular, yet warm-hearted, strong-minded man, with a hatred of cant and humbug in every form, a thorough believer in the ultimate winnowing out of all the chaff and rubbish infesting society, and in the perfection of humanity by a close adherence to the great natural laws and forces regulating, through Divine wisdom, the universe."

Perhaps these words would also be a fair description of Anthony Hewitson?

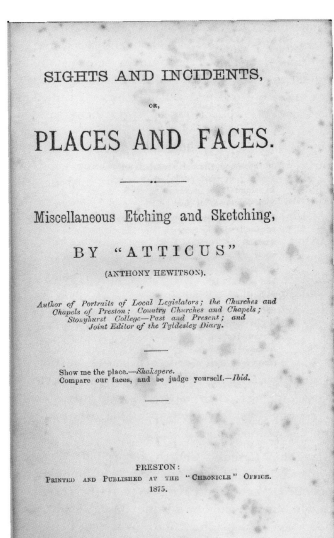

SIGHTS AND INCIDENTS,

OR,

PLACES AND FACES.

Miscellaneous Etching and Sketching,

BY "ATTICUS"

(ANTHONY HEWITSON),

Author of Portraits of Local Legislators; the Churches and Chapels of Preston; Country Churches and Chapels; Stonyhurst College—Past and Present; and Joint Editor of the Tyldesley Diary.

Show me the place.—*Shakspere.*
Compare our faces, and be judge yourself.—*Ibid.*

PRESTON:
PRINTED AND PUBLISHED AT THE "CHRONICLE" OFFICE.
1875.